Brain Power

Vernon Mark,
M.D., F.A.C.S.
with Jeffrey P. Mark,
M.Sc.

Brain Power

———

*A Neurosurgeon's
Complete Program to
Maintain and Enhance
Brain Fitness
Throughout Your Life*

Houghton Mifflin Company
Boston 1989

For information about permission to reproduce selections from this
book, write to Permissions, Houghton Mifflin Company, 2 Park
Street, Boston, Massachusetts 02108.

Library of Congress Cataloging-in-Publication Data

Mark, Vernon H., date.
  Brain power : a neurosurgeon's complete program to maintain and
enhance brain fitness throughout your life / Vernon Mark with
Jeffrey P. Mark.
      p.   cm.
  Bibliography: p.
  Includes index.
  ISBN 0-395-49861-9
    1. Alzheimer's disease — Prevention. 2. Brain — Aging.
3. Brain — Diseases — Prevention. 4. Mental health
I. Mark, J. Paul. II. Title.
RC523.M36   1989   89-7520
616.8'045 — dc20   CIP

Printed in the United States of America

Q 10 9 8 7 6 5 4 3 2 1

All the information presented as case histories and stories in *Brain
Power* is medically accurate. However, all names, places, and individual characteristics that could identify specific people have been
changed to protect privacy. Any resemblance to persons living or dead
is coincidental.

Before you start the regimens presented in this book, consult your
own physician to make sure that they are suitable for you.

None of the information presented here is intended to substitute for
medical advice. If you have any problems or questions related to your
own health and fitness, you should direct them to your physician.

To My Wife, Alexandra

———

For L.S.B. from J.P.M.

Acknowledgments

It would have been impossible to write a book such as this without the help of literally hundreds of dedicated men and women who taught me what I know about medicine and the brain. Whatever wisdom and information I am able to impart to others on these subjects is directly attributable to their efforts. To all my colleagues, both past and present, in the medical profession, I can only offer a woefully inadequate thank you.

I'd like to say a special thanks to my partner, colleague, and close friend of twenty-five years, Dr. Thomas D. Sabin. It's been an honor and a joy to work with Tom. Our crusade first began as a result of his efforts, and his unflagging energy fortified me when I most needed it.

My sincere gratitude also goes out to the following individuals who have supported me and my research during the past forty years. Truly I have been blessed to have had so many gifted people to work with: Dr. William Sweet, Dr. Ray Adams, Dr. James White, Dr. Frank Ervin, Dr. Tom Kemper, Dr. Owen Wangenstein, Dr. Derek Denny-Brown, Dr. Tom Hackett, Dr. Norman Geschwind, Dr. Myron Rosenthal, Dr. A. T. Rassmussen, Dr. Barry Campbell, Dr. Ernst Gellhorn, Dr. A. B. Baker, Dr. Paul Yakovlev, Dr. William V. McDermott, Dr. Janice Stevens, Dr. Jonathan Lieff, Dr. Al Gruber, Dr. Donald Davidoff, Dr. Anthony DeStefano, and Mr. Paul McPherson. Mr. John Kimball also provided invaluable support.

All the work that I've been able to accomplish at Sabin & Mark and the Center for Memory Impairment and Neurobehavioral Disorders (CMIND) for so long would not have been possible without the collaborative efforts of an outstanding group. Joyce Sabin supported and guided the enterprises through many difficult obstacles. Elec Toth, with great technical expertise and a wonderful sense of humor, kept us all together. Mary Grace Neal and Forrest Eastman have both given invaluable assistance.

This book would never have become a reality without the perseverance and sage advice of Flip Brophy of Sterling Lord Literistic. Jeff and I are both keenly aware of and grateful for her outstanding abilities. Also, Barbara Hoffman gave us some timely advice and helpful suggestions that greatly improved the readability of the manuscript.

Finally, I'd like to recognize the heroic efforts of Mrs. Ruth Hapgood. I'm well aware that few authors are privileged to work with an editor with such talent and vision.

All errors in fact or judgment are exclusively my own.

Contents

PART III

A Complete Program for Building and Rebuilding Brain Power Energy

PART IV

Brain Power in the 1990s and Beyond

Introduction:
New Challenges

Almost everyone has a turning point in his life, and I've had mine. It came about nearly a decade ago when I realized that my hope of making a fundamental discovery in medicine was no longer likely. My research support, which had continued for more than thirty-four years, was winding down, and my fifteen-year directorship of the neurosurgical service of Boston City Hospital had become routine. I was bored with the rarefied atmosphere of academic medicine, in which patients are referred to by their diseases rather than by their names and where surgical outcomes are measured by mortality statistics rather than by improvements in the quality of life. That's when I decided to go back to practicing medicine the way I had when I first left medical school, assuming once again a one-to-one relationship with my patients.

These changes in my professional life were accompanied by changes in my personal life too. My own feelings of invulnerability, and even immortality, which shielded me from the harsh realities of treating patients with cancerous brain tumors, end-stage malignancy with intractable pain, and devastating head injuries — the woof and warp of most neurosurgical practices — began to erode. Oh, I was feeling fine, keeping my weight down, running a mile or two every day, and looking forward to the golden years.

Then I started visiting residents in nursing homes around the greater Boston area. I began to see people who looked just like me, only ten, twenty, or thirty years older. They also ate well, kept their weight down, and did exercises and all the other things their doctors recommended. Their hearts and lungs were going strong; they were living — or, rather, existing — inside an institution. Unfortunately, their brains didn't keep pace with the rest of their bodies. Most of them sat apathetically watching television or staring into space. Sometimes they or their neighbors became noisy. The golden years had turned into years of boredom and hopelessness.

Occasionally, I was surprised to see someone in a nursing home whom I had known professionally. Doris, an eighty-three-year-old urologist, had been a professor at a major medical school and had become slightly but continuously disoriented. Now when she walked down the nursing home corridor and saw a medical chart rack, her old conditioned reflexes clicked into place. She would wheel the chart rack into the nearest room containing male patients and attempt to examine them. When the residents recognized that she herself had on only a johnny, which was deficient in back, their protests would bring the nurses running.

Then there were the two little old men who sought me out, tiptoeing into my examining room hand in hand, frightened and quite unsure of themselves. One of the men had been a family physician for more than forty years on Cape Cod, and the other had been a professor of biochemistry and had written important books on metabolism. I discovered that they always held hands because they were disoriented and often got lost in the corridors. They didn't want to become separated, so they took courage from each other in trying to find their way back to familiar surroundings.

Like the haunting refrain from an old popular song, the question kept running through my head, "Is that all there is?"

In contrast to the bustling activity of the teaching hospitals where I worked, the nursing home wards were quiet and slow-paced. The patients moved slowly. The staff needed a great deal of patience to take their histories because they answered so slowly or sometimes not at all. Doctors had no chance to see a lot of patients in a short time and make rapid and dramatic decisions. In fact, just examining one patient took more than an hour, not because the problems were difficult but because the patient's movements, reactions, and answers came so slowly.

Working in nursing homes changed the course of my life and my approach to medicine. I realized that it was a waste of human competence and wisdom to incarcerate elderly citizens in human warehouses for the remainder of their lives. What a tragedy to have broken up the extended family with its traditions and values. Somehow, I knew I had to try to keep elderly people from going into nursing homes or into colonies consisting only of elderly people or into conglomerate housing only for the elderly. Of course, to keep people from going into nursing homes, we have to do those things that will keep their brain power working as well as possible and that will prevent brain disease, brain injury, and brain poisoning from sending them prematurely to the nursing home.

Metropolitan Boston, with a population of about three and a half million, contains more than two hundred nursing homes. When I visited the country of Costa Rica a few years ago, I was told there were only four nursing homes for a population of three million. Where were the elderly? They were with their families.

Of course, Costa Rica is not a wealthy country, its citizens have a shorter life expectancy, and it doesn't offer many of the advantages that we have in the United States. But it does have something we lack — the extended family. There, unlike here, older people are valued members of their families.

In this country we're so concerned about paying for medical

care that we forget our priorities. At least one public official has recommended that we keep costly treatments away from elderly patients so that they can die more quickly and not be a burden to society. My approach is just the opposite. I say, let's treat the elderly, and even the not so elderly, so that they can avoid the situation in which expensive end-stage treatments are necessary. And let's keep them functioning and a part of the extended family.

This task is not glamorous, and it doesn't involve basic research or the possibility of new frontiers in science or medicine, reasons that most doctors avoid pursuing it. It requires a lot of patience and stick-to-itiveness, not only on the part of doctors and nurses but on the part of everyone who takes care of those with declining mental abilities.

I've found, however, that the most difficult patients to deal with are often the ones who have the best chances for recovery. Sam was an Armenian immigrant who married his childhood sweetheart shortly after he came to this country. He and his wife worked hard at the large and prosperous fur business they established. They had one daughter, who married and had children, and they led a rather idyllic life until Sam's wife died.

Sam kept managing the business, however, until one day he got sick and went to the hospital for treatment of a heart condition. Some of the medicine he was given caused him to become somewhat disoriented and noisy. As a result, his doctors put him on another medication to stop his disturbances, which were keeping other people in the hospital ward awake at night. By the time he was ready to be discharged, Sam was totally disoriented and incontinent. A social worker and Sam's daughter thought that he could be cared for only in a nursing home, so he was admitted to one and his medication was increased again when he started to get noisy. He was given so much medicine that in his disoriented state he fell down and broke his hip. When he came out of the hospital after hip surgery, he was even more incoherent and required still more medication. His daughter couldn't deal with the reality of her father's problems, so she provided a substantial amount of money to have him taken care of, gave the nursing home an incorrect address and phone number, and left town.

When I saw him, I discovered that Sam was taking too much medication, and I gradually decreased his dosage. The nursing staff protested, saying he would become noisy and disruptive again. I said, "Let's put him in a separate room, with just one other patient who won't be disturbed by him, far away from everyone else. If he gets loud, no one will notice." In a few weeks, Sam returned almost to normal — until he discovered that his daughter had abandoned him. Then he took on all the symptoms of his roommate, a man who had advanced Alzheimer's disease. From my knowledge of Sam's case, I was sure that his symptoms of Alzheimer's must have been due to something else. With the help of a psychiatrist, I got treatment for him and finally he did return to normal.

Sam suffered from a combination of brain poisoning and depression; both are treatable conditions. He didn't need to be in a nursing home, and when I discovered that fact I set out to find his daughter and to help him reconstruct his life.

Cases like Sam's give me an appreciation of the potential of patients who seem to be intractably demented. I realize that when a doctor makes a diagnosis it usually sounds as if it came from Moses; but doctors are far from infallible. "Never give up hope." That's what I tell myself when I see a patient with a diagnosis of brain disease. I may be looking at another Sam.

Since I began discovering lost members of society in nursing homes and helping them return to active lives, I've realized that many people can be saved from such an ordeal if they understand and follow a simple axiom:

Behavior is always the result of brain-environment interaction.

The brain in this instance includes not only the structure and function of the central nervous system but also its internal environment — the support it receives from the other organ systems in the body. Environment refers not just to the ongoing sensory impulses received by the brain and their modification by a person's behavior, but also to the stored, vivid memories of past environment and the person's expectations for the future.

This axiom is not an example of mind-body or brain-environment dualism since the two elements, brain and environment, are so continuously and inextricably intertwined that they are inseparable. What the axiom tells us is that altered behavior doesn't just happen — something in the environment or in the brain makes it happen. Sam didn't just become demented; the drugs his doctors gave him made him appear that way.

The most important organ systems in the human body are the brain and the heart. When heart muscle cells die, they don't regenerate because there is no replacement mechanism. More important, when brain cells die, there are no replacement brain cells to maintain the integrity of the brain.

To a certain extent, the plasticity of brain function allows for accommodation when small amounts of brain tissue are lost because of injury or stroke. This plasticity accounts for the fact that sometimes function is recovered after a stroke produces a loss of speech or limb weakness. The heart, too, has enough reserve to survive when some muscle is lost following a coronary artery occlusion (obstruction). However, when a major portion of cardiac muscle is infarcted (killed through lack of blood supply), heart function can be totally shut down.

The heart is essentially just a mechanical pump, and someday in the not too distant future we will be able to devise an artificial one that will work, even in the face of a massive coronary artery occlusion. The almost magical functions that are encompassed within our craniums, however, will never be artificially duplicated. When essential portions of the brain are destroyed, there is simply no way to re-create them.

You need to know two key points if you want to maximize your brain power: First, you must keep the loss of your brain cells down to an absolute minimum, and second, you must practice those things that enhance the functions of your remaining brain cells and tissue. Once learned and applied, the lessons that neurological science teaches can give real benefits to all.

I will teach you these lessons that improve and maintain brain power. I'll also explain how to avoid losing brain cells. Ultimately, how well you follow through will determine the success of the program. The choice is yours to make.

Part I

The Principles of Preserving Brain Power

Chapter 1

Brain Power:
The Key to the
Quality of Life

Y ou've been taught to believe that if you take care of your body the way most doctors advise — by exercising regularly, eating the proper foods, staying away from cigarettes, drugs, and alcohol — you will live a long and productive life. You may even believe that doing those healthy things will keep you going strong well into your ninth decade. Unfortunately, that's not quite true.

During the past nine years, I have visited dozens of nursing homes of all kinds and have found remarkable similarities between residents who were not previously in mental hospitals. For the most part they had led quite healthy lives and had not been drug addicts or alcoholics. They had not abused their bodies. They had eaten moderately, had taken plenty of exercise, and had managed to live successfully into their eighth or ninth decade. In short, these were people who had done everything right. How, then, did nearly all of them end their lives not as productive, functioning individuals but as dead weight to society?

More than 90 percent of all the long-term nursing home patients I have seen have a moderate to severe loss of intellectual function. No matter what put them in nursing homes in the first place, what kept them there was not poor function of their hearts, livers, or kidneys. By living carefully (such as by not smoking) they often avoided many of the cancers that killed off their peers ten or twenty years earlier. And many of them had survived the death of a spouse who was stricken prematurely by a heart attack. What confined these survivors to nursing homes was that in growing older they had lost brain power.

For decades, doctors have advised Americans on how to live longer, healthier lives, and that advice has had a dramatic effect on all of us. Average life spans have risen steadily; the incidence of heart disease is declining; certain cancer rates are also dropping. We're eating more fiber-rich foods, avoiding saturated fats, watching our HDLs and LDLs, and doing plenty of stressful exercises. We're also filling up nursing homes in record numbers.

There's something fundamentally wrong with medical advice that tells people how to live longer but at the same time condemns them to decades of meaningless life. Confronting this contradictory evidence for the first time, if I were a thirty-, forty-, or fifty-year-old carefully following a doctor's health, diet, and exercise regimen, I'd have to ask myself, "What am I saving myself for? After all, who wants to finish life in a depressing institution staring blankly into space? Wouldn't it be preferable to go out in a blaze of glory, a cigarette in one hand and a cherry liqueur–centered chocolate in the other?"

True, no one has ever won a prize for having the healthiest heart, liver, kidneys, or pancreas in a home for the aged. But before you discard all that good medical advice you've gotten over the years, let me tell you what its one basic flaw is: You can have a perfectly healthy pancreas, liver, kidney, and intestines, but if your brain isn't functioning the quality of your life will be zero.

Keeping your heart and lungs strong and healthy will not guarantee that your brain will remain completely functional. It is healthy brain function alone that ensures your ability to master and control your environment.

Many people with missing limbs go on living quite successfully with relatively minor adjustments. Recent advances in medicine have allowed us to replace the liver, the lungs, and the heart with transplants. However, a single tiny, destructive lesion in the brainstem (the neural tissue that connects the large brain to the spinal cord) can produce irreversible coma. An individual who suffers this fate will continue to breathe, have a blood pressure, and circulate blood; the liver and bowels will function; but the person will be in a vegetative state — a life without meaning. The brain is the one essential organ that we cannot do without. It is our identity; it cannot be replaced.

If your goal is to live to be ninety or one hundred, I suggest you follow your doctor's advice to the letter. It's not the most exciting way to live, but it's the surest way we now know for surviving in the long term. I believe, however, that survival by itself is not something worth aspiring to. Without the full use of a healthy brain, or the expectation of recovering lost brain power, life really isn't worth living.

No matter what else may be wrong physically, a fully functioning brain gives you the chance to control and shape the environment around you. The degree of control is proportional to the talents, skills, and abilities you've developed in your brain over a lifetime and how intensively you use them. I once treated a man with cerebral palsy whose disease was so severe that he had violent, uncontrollable movement abnormalities and as a result was confined to a wheelchair. He was unable to feed himself or even to take care of his simplest needs. Nevertheless, he earned a master's degree in computer engineering and went on to become the president of a computer company. His brain function, apart from his disease, was excellent. It allowed him to lead a meaningful, rich life.

THE HEALTHY BRAIN

To help you understand how optimal brain functioning comes about and why the diets, exercises, and regimens I prescribe later in this book do work, I will be bringing you some of the new research that isn't yet a part of general knowledge or preventive practice. My objective is not to confuse you with obscure and technical information. I want you to come away with an understanding of what you can usefully do to strengthen your own brain power so that you will have more incentive to stay with the program.

The basic functions of healthy brain power are determined by four things: first, the physical structure of the brain and its chemical environment; second, the moment-to-moment information received by the brain from the outside world and the rest of the body; third, the information stored from past experience; and fourth, the associations made in the brain between present and past information.

All four factors are interrelated and interdependent. The physical structure of the brain, for example, is shaped by experiences. Unlike muscles, which can only grow in size with use, brain structure changes in billions of complex ways through continual interaction with both external and internal environments. But without proper stimulation, development and function are interrupted.

A clear demonstration of how environment shapes brain structure was an animal experiment done many years ago. Newborn cats were raised in a laboratory in total darkness. In all other respects their rearing was normal: They had food, water, exercise, and interactions with other cats and humans. Under conditions of total darkness, the visual pathways in their brains did not develop, and a microscopic examination showed that some of the nerve cells in those pathways were dead. Up to a certain age the pathways retained a capacity to develop and the animals were able to see when light was restored. But after that age the changes in the brain structure produced by environment were permanent.

Similarly, infant monkeys raised in an abnormal way, deprived of their own mothers and other living monkeys, grew up to be incurable deviants. A hot water bottle, the sound of a ticking clock, and ample food that was provided mechanically simply did not offer enough significant environmental stimuli to allow important parts of their brains to develop normally.

Such experiments have many implications for humans. They show that environment plays a large role in brain power and function. To reach your maximum potential, you have to be aware of how important environment is. Do you really think you could live in a place that is devoid of stimuli and expect to lead a productive, healthy life?

I once treated a nursing home patient named Louise who had been confined to bed for several years, was partially blind, and could see only to one side of her head and not to the other. In medical terms she had a defect called homonomous hemianopsia. Louise's condition was caused by a stroke that destroyed brain tissue and made her more susceptible to losing intellectual function. She had spent two years living in an alcove in such a position that the functional part of her vision was turned to a blank wall and the blind part was turned to the outside world.

Her doctors thought that her mental abilities were severely diminished. In fact, she simply had no new visual environment — just the bare walls all day long — which, compounded with the brain loss she had suffered, made her seem and act demented. When I discovered her problem and had her turned around so that she could see the outside world, she underwent a remarkable improvement. Her withdrawn behavior had been brought on by a lack of meaningful visual stimuli, which exacerbated the effects of her stroke.

New and stimulating surroundings are just one of many environmental factors that can contribute to improved brain function. When nothing interesting or challenging happens, however, those factors stop contributing to the normal environment and the result is changes in brain function. Many of the changes in Louise's mental status brought on by her decreased visual environment were reversible. Over time, the changes would have become permanent.

It is true that in normal people a significant number of brain cells die every year and do not regenerate. Some people have inferred from this scientific information that after a certain point many elderly (or even not so elderly) people begin to develop mental deficiencies, presumably from the observed cell death. Taking this a step further, some have suggested that the loss of brain cells produces senility, which they perceive as a *normal* consequence of aging. That inference, however, is wrong.

What most people do not realize is that compensatory changes take place in our brains as we get older. Yes, we do lose brain cells every year of our lives and, yes, if we live long enough there is some shrinkage in overall brain mass. However, two factors that occur in the normal, healthy brain compensate for the slow tissue loss.

First, the sheath around the fibers that carry nerve impulses away from the nerve cells becomes thicker with a fatty substance called myelin. The thickening of the myelin sheath is correlated with *increasing* function throughout life. When an infant or very young child begins to sit up or walk, the myelin sheath first begins to thicken, increasing the efficiency of the transmission of electrical signals in the brain.

The second compensating factor is that the fibers that bring impulses to the brain develop more branches, producing improved communication between all remaining cells. The better your brain cells communicate with each other, the better able you are to do the mental and physical things you want. So to set the record straight, senility is definitely *not* a consequence of normal aging.

To understand why some people become senile and what can

be done to prevent that condition from happening, we need to understand both the variety of common problems that are routinely mistaken for senility and the real signs and symptoms of senility. The latter are factors related to abnormal brain function. Remember that there should be constant improvement in some brain functions through the eighth decade of life, as long as the brain is normal. Don't make the mistake of believing certain misinformed physicians who claim that everyone is ultimately destined to become senile. It just isn't so.

As you learn about your own brain's function, you will be better able psychologically to deal with the fact of aging. You'll know that when brain function begins to fail it is not a sign of old age. Instead, it is a sign of disease, injury, or neglect. It is a warning signal that something is wrong that needs to be fixed.

With the information you'll learn in the coming chapters, you'll be able to work as a fully informed partner with a medical professional if you or someone you love needs one. If you can't fix the problem yourself, this book will show you where and how to get the help you need. Just as important, the programs outlined here will tell you how to prevent certain things from going wrong and how to find out what's wrong, if anything. We start by telling you how to examine someone else if the need arises and then how to test yourself.

Chapter 2

Brain Power Tests
That You Can Do Alone
or with Someone Else

How can you tell if you have normal brain power? The problem is more difficult than you might first suppose. Medically, the word *normal* can have a broad range of interpretations. To complicate things even more, many people have learned ways to hide or mask their declining brain power.

Margaret, an eighty-year-old woman I met in a nursing home, appeared at first glance to be alert and in good health. When I walked over to her she greeted me by saying, "Hello, Doctor. How are you? I'm feeling just fine." When I asked her questions, she always responded affirmatively with answers such as "I'm fine" or "Yes, fine."

Faced with these kinds of responses and Margaret's apparent good health, Margaret's doctor of eight years had found no reason to do a detailed neurological evaluation. At first, I didn't see much reason to doubt her mental abilities either, until a few simple questions turned up inconsistencies.

When I asked her what the date was, she was able to correctly tell me it was a Tuesday, but she had no idea what month or day of the month it was, and she had absolutely no idea what year it was. I asked her to tell me what city she was in and she replied, "Hartford, Connecticut." That turned out to be her home as a child, but her nursing home was actually in a suburb of Boston.

It is not uncommon for certain individuals, like Margaret, to have thin social facades that are both practiced and facile. They carry on light conversations, respond to questions, and make themselves appear quite normal. However, they are in most other ways profoundly demented. Because they seem normal and consider themselves to be normal, their problems go undiagnosed for long periods of time.

The blame for failing to identify neurological problems earlier in their progress lies to a great extent with the medical profession. Many doctors who are excellent diagnosticians in other areas of the body don't feel comfortable diagnosing problems of the brain, particularly those that relate to higher brain function. Their reluctance is unfortunate because many simple tests exist that can determine substantial deficits and that can be carried out not only by physicians but also by laypeople.

You are about to learn a few of the tests that I conduct. Some require assistance but many you can do by yourself. The tests are trip wires; they do not automatically provide a diagnosis, but they will alert you to the presence of a problem and, perhaps, to the need for expert assessment by a trained physician or psychologist. Later, we'll take a closer look at the symptoms of neurological deficits as determined by these tests and others and I will explain how to interpret them.

MENTAL STATUS EXAMS

Appendix 1 contains two kinds of mental status exams — one for you to give someone else and one for you to try yourself. Here I discuss each part of the test that you can administer to someone else.

Mental Inventory

Before I start my examination, I take a careful look at my subject. Does he seem unusually sloppy in appearance or older than his chronological years? Is he unable to sit still and, if so, are his movements voluntary or involuntary? Something as small as a nervous tic can indicate a brain malfunction known as dyskinesia.

The most basic and fundamental tests of brain power involve taking inventory of a person's ability to move body parts (arms, legs, the muscles of the face) and to speak. Any type of paralysis of limbs or any obvious abnormality of speech usually indicates profound loss of brain function. Those features are, of course, readily observable and rarely go unnoticed by either the person having the symptoms or those around him.

It is important to know that conditions such as paralysis, or even blindness or deafness, complicate the job of discovering less obvious kinds of deficits. The basic mental status tests depend on the ability of the subject to hear, see, and speak and to move his or her limbs, tongue, and lips. If your subject leads an active life and is not aware of having any of the conditions I just described, there probably isn't any need for you to concern yourself with hidden medical conditions that may confound the test results.

Mental status tests always begin with orientation questions: "Can you tell me who you are?" "Where are you?" "What year is this?" An inability to precisely answer these types of questions indicates a profound loss of intellectual ability. I sometimes ask my patients to write down exactly where they were within the past twenty-four hours and at what times they went to different places. "When did you wake up?" "When did you have breakfast?" "Where did you go shopping?" "Are there large gaps in your schedule with unaccounted-for time?" "Can you remember with whom you spoke and about what subjects?" These are the types of questions I ask. Patients' inability to recall what they did yesterday or where they were at particular times indicates a potential problem.

Speech and Language

This part of the exam evaluates the speech centers of the brain. Many neurologists use the repetition of the following sentence to test for language deficits: "No ifs, ands, or buts." If you're testing yourself, you should look away from the page and repeat the sentence from memory. Simple? Yes, simple for the normal individual. If your test subject speaks English and can't repeat that sentence correctly and fluently, it means trouble. The person should not hesitate and should not slur the words.

Take out a newspaper or magazine and have your subject read a few words — a short sentence — aloud. Then have him or her write out the sentence word for word from memory. Failure to do either of these things accurately is cause for further investigation.

Next, point to objects such as a pen, ring, bracelet, or watch and ask the person to name the objects without pausing. I often finish a series such as this with the metal clasp of my watchband. This is a difficult object to name, and I often get a variety of incorrect responses including "lock," "hinge," "claps," or "the thing you close the band with." Any of those responses indicates diminished naming abilities. By itself, poor performance on this test may not be critical; however, depending on other factors, it may be part of a pattern of deficiency.

As I give tests of the speech center of the brain, I increase the difficulty of the questions. After the naming of inanimate objects, I test animate naming abilities, which is also a test of verbal fluency. I might ask, for example, "How many animals can you name in a minute?" If someone can't come up with at least fifteen to twenty animals in that time, I usually suspect a language disorder known as anomic aphasia. The disorder may be more difficult to detect if the subject gets between twelve and fifteen correct responses, but a score of between five and ten indicates some sort of aphasia, or loss of language ability.

The last question in this part of the test asks the subject to spell the word *world* backward. Many people with even minimal brain problems, such as brain poisoning from alcohol or drugs, will not be able to complete this test successfully because it requires the use of higher brain functions in the language hemisphere that are easily disrupted.

You can demonstrate to yourself and others how alcohol suppresses the language function in the brain by conducting this test at a party where the guests have had many alcoholic drinks. If they don't have a chance to practice, some people will not be able to do the exercise successfully. In the absence of any intoxication, or brain poisoning, failing this test could be significant.

Motor Functions

You can perform a short test of motor functions by giving your subject simple "crossover" commands such as putting his right hand on his left ear and vice versa. People with severe and extensive abnormalities in the language center of the brain often cannot do crossover tasks. Deep lesions in the midline thalamic brain structures can produce a similar syndrome. I also ask the person to show me how he can use his hands to complete simple tasks, such as combing his hair and tying the laces of his shoes. If he can't do these things, he has apraxia, the inability to perform meaningful skilled movements. This may involve abnormalities of both language and motor parts of the brain.

Higher Intellectual Abilities

To test the function of the frontal lobe, a part of the brain that controls executive functions, I give the following test of hand movements. First I ask the subject to make a fist and to use his fist to strike a table or armrest with one hand. Then I ask him to open his hand and hit the table or armrest with the open palm of the other hand. Finally, I ask him to alternate between using his fist with one hand and palm with the other ten times in rapid succession. Then I tell him to reverse the hands. If the subject makes a mistake the first time, I give him a second chance. A failure both times is very important to note.

Simple mental arithmetic is the next area to test in the mental status exam. As a warm-up, ask your subject simple problems such as subtracting 16 from 100. If he comes up with 86, he's probably not concentrating. Multiplication tables rather than simple arithmetic are also used to test long-term memory. I usually take people at least one step past the twelves: "If $12 \times 12 = 144$, then what is 13×12?" If the person tries to picture the numbers and do a written multiplication in his mind he really doesn't have a clear idea of the basic meaning of multiplication — that it is simply a shorthand way of doing addition. What I test for here is not only the ability to do simple mathematical problems but also an understanding of the numerical process.

You must be careful when testing a person's math skills to be certain that the tests are carried out at the correct level. If someone has no schooling, math skills may be deficient without indicating loss of brain function. Proficiency in math is relative, which I came to understand more clearly when I tested a twenty-eight-year-old graduate student in mathematics at the Massachusetts Institute of Technology who received an injury to his head.

This young man's chief complaint was that he experienced severe headaches. As for his math abilities, however, he could do problems of much greater difficulty in his head than I. As it turned out, the young mathematician's brain had a bilateral blood clot, which I subsequently removed. His math skills, which I thought were excellent before the operation, actually improved significantly after surgery according to his peers at MIT.

A different kind of test that has specific implications for other types of higher brain function is called proverb interpretation. I mention several well-known proverbs and ask the person to tell me what they mean: "A rolling stone gathers no moss." "A stitch in time saves nine." "A person who lives in a glass house shouldn't throw stones."

Someone who is deficient in this area will, for example, interpret the glass house proverb literally as meaning that if you throw stones at a glass house you'll break the glass. Often the mistake of interpreting a proverb literally is the first sign of dementing disease in an educated person. For that reason, this is a very simple but useful test to give someone who is suspected of loss of mental ability.

Occasionally I see someone who in other respects appears demented but who interprets a proverb correctly. Since severely demented people are incapable of the type of reasoning required by this test, a correct response to the test in conjunction with other problems leads me to suspect a form of depression rather than dementia.

Another series of tests that helps me sharpen my analysis of higher brain function involves asking the subject to draw a series of pictures, starting with the face of a clock. If all the numbers have been put on one side, for example, that indicates one further avenue to investigate. The inversion of numbers likewise indicates another kind of follow-up test.

Constructional abilities can be tested by having the subject copy or reproduce drawings of increasing complexity. For example, I hand the person a sheet of paper that has drawings of simple shapes on the left and I ask the person to copy the shapes on the right-hand side of the page. Then I grade the person's drawings for accuracy.

Next I ask the subject to draw a three-dimensional picture of an object such as a house or a flowerpot, and I grade this picture for accuracy as well.

Long-Term Memory

Long-term memories are stored in several anatomically separate parts of the brain, and the test I use to measure the intactness of this function is of either American geography or American presidents. Public schools have generally stopped teaching geography, so I find that most younger people have trouble in that area. Most people, however, should have no problem naming the current president of the United States and the preceding four, in reverse order. My experience is that normal individuals do occasionally skip either Gerald Ford or Jimmy Carter, but with minimal prompting they are able to recall the name. It is highly suspect, however, whenever someone cannot remember the name of the incumbent.

The last test of brain power in this short exam is to give the subject a list of three or four unrelated words and ask him to recall the words, in their exact order, at the end of four minutes. When you administer this test, it is important not to just say the words, wait four minutes without distraction, and ask the subject to repeat them. Almost everyone can do that, including motivated people with deficient short-term memories. They will simply repeat the words over and over to themselves silently during the four-minute interval. In the mental status exams I give, however, repetition of the words is impossible because I give the subject a math problem or keep him distracted with other kinds of questions.

The three-word sequences I use most often are "door, window, and mirror" or "horse, banana, and Chevrolet." If the subject is concentrating, he can be expected to get three out of three. If he is not, then two out of three is still acceptable. Anything less usually indicates that a problem exists and that further tests are necessary.

The battery of tests I just described really only scratches the surface in each area. I give patients longer and more sophisticated tests when they fail some of these simple tests. It doesn't mean the tests here aren't useful just because they are simple. If a subject is putting forth a good, consistent effort, is paying attention and concentrating, and does not pass these tests with flying colors, then a problem certainly exists that should be investigated.

I have one caution to offer about the content and format of this type of examination. The questions and their order should be changed whenever the same test is given to different people who might communicate with each other. Several years ago, I conducted tests like the ones described here to all the residents of a nursing home. I saw most of the first-floor residents in the morning and examined several people on the second floor that evening. When I returned the next day, I found that the first few people I tested performed dramatically better than expected.

Since I had found that more than 90 percent of nursing home residents have obvious trouble with these simple tests, I had to ask myself in this case why there was such a difference from one day to the next. Indeed, the first patient I saw that morning, a woman who had had bifrontal lobotomies in her childhood, an operation that supposedly took away her ability to plan and organize, did remarkably well on the tests. I knew that something was amiss, but it wasn't until I saw my fifth patient that I discovered what had happened.

The fifth person was a man who, like the other four, did better than expected until he began stumbling over the test phrase "No ifs, ands, or buts." After a few unsuccessful attempts, he took a file card out of his pocket, turned his back to me, and began practicing the phrase. From him, I discovered that one of the residents who had taken the tests the previous day had coached the second-floor residents on the test until they had all the answers down pat. Of course, if the nursing home residents had really been trying to hide their problems, they were unlikely to succeed. No amount of coaching can conceal the loss of brain power from an astute neurologist.

While the tests here do not represent a complete neurological exam and cannot identify seizure or movement disorders, various losses of sensation, or partial losses of vision, they are extremely valuable. In subsequent chapters you will learn about more sophisticated tests done with x-rays as well as about some symptoms to look for in people with declining brain power. With a conscientious effort, you should be able to test yourself periodically to make certain that you are maintaining control over your own environment.

Now, without turning back, can you recall one of the three word sequences I gave earlier? Check yourself. If you don't score 100 percent on that and all the other tests, we'll explore what that could mean.

Chapter 3

What the
Examination Means
t to Do About It

walked into the solarium of the pavil-
jured patients at the Massachusetts
l and I overheard two young men in
he first man, who was wearing a white
, said, "Hey, guess what! I just got a
and the guy told me my stock portfo-
roof! I'm not only a multimillionaire,
n, a tall, hollow-eyed, and emaciated
dly by saying, "That's nice. But what
l to me? I completed the most success-
:ompany's history and they've decided
ve vice president. Next year I'm in line

both were severely incapacitated and
weeks in the hospital, I might have be-
But the patient with his head bandaged
morrhage in the deep anterior portion
of his brain from an accident that had required surgery. And the
tall, emaciated man had a pronounced thiamine (B_1) deficiency

related to his chronic alcohol abuse. He suffered from Korsakoff's psychosis. They were both, for different reasons, completely disoriented, and neither had the ability to remember recent events or conversations. Consequently, they kept themselves
spellbound by telling one incredible story after another. Since
neither could remember anything for more than a minute, everything they said to one another seemed to them to be completely plausible.

A most striking feature about these two men was that, although they had similar symptoms of short-term memory loss,
their diagnoses were markedly different. The man with the brain
hemorrhage had had part of the anterior deep portion of his
brain destroyed. The second man had destroyed part of a structure deep in his brain known as the thalamus by failing to take in
enough vitamin B_1. Although their problems were different, each
man failed the same part of the mental status exam.

So two people can appear to have the same kind of problem
by the results of the exam, but the exam cannot differentiate
between underlying causes. Until recently, when neurologists
and neurosurgeons began using CAT scanning technology (CAT
stands for "computerized axial tomography"), the only way to
diagnose a brain disease was with the use of a mental status
exam, a neurological exam, and a good hunch. Sadly, the other
x-ray tests of the brain were risky and often not decisive, and the
only sure way we were able to confirm a neurologic disease was
by brain surgery or by looking at brain sections during a brain
autopsy.

PROFILE OF MEMORY LOSS

If you've just given the mental status exam to a friend, relative,
or loved one or have taken it yourself and have identified one or
more problems with memory, you won't be able to make a posi-

tive diagnosis. But by looking at a number of common signs and symptoms, you may be able to *rule out* the presence of certain diseases.

Suppose that you or your subject passed everything except the recent-memory part of the exam. What could cause that to happen? A patient of mine who had had a deep portion of her brain called the fornix sectioned in the process of evacuating a brain tumor had that kind of memory problem. She was able to carry on a perfectly rational discussion so long as her recent memory wasn't tested and so long as there was no interruption in the continuity of the conversation. But if I left the room, even for as little as thirty seconds, she had no memory of my previous visit and was completely mystified when I came back into the room and tried to remind her of our previous conversation.

The disruption of the inner portion of the temporal lobes, called the hippocampi, produces a similar syndrome. Some years ago, a surgeon unwittingly removed both hippocampi in a patient with severe brain abnormalities, and the outcome was a catastrophic loss of recent memory. (Fortunately, the case has been reported many times in the medical literature to prevent a repetition of that disastrous medical result.)

I have also seen patients who had extensive injuries to the ventral and posteriomedial portions of the thalamus that produced both a loss of recent memory and also a loss of remote memory so great that not only would they forget who had been the U.S. president in a previous term, but they would also forget the meanings of words that they had previously known. The most pitiable case I ever saw of this kind was a man who had a deep thalamic hemorrhage. While he appeared lucid at times, he gradually worsened to the point where he could no longer remember people he had met, including his own wife and children.

In sum, if you administered the mental status exam and your subject got a below-average score on short-term (or recent) memory, the cause may well be due to a problem with the thalamus, the hippocampus, or the fornix. However, the people I just described with short-term memory problems also had other medical symptoms such as blackouts and disorientation. If no other signs or symptoms of brain loss are present, it's less likely that deep brain structures are involved in the cause of such symptoms.

In the final analysis, the kind, severity, and duration of memory loss is dependent on the location of the brain damage, the extent of the damage and its cause (injury, tumor, vitamin deficiency, stroke). Each case has to be evaluated individually to determine the best treatment and prognosis.

RECOVERING LOST MEMORY

Sometimes a loss of short-term memory is reversible, for reasons that physicians have not been able to explain. A retired farmer once came to me because he had episodes in which he lost all memory for several hours. During these periods he became confused and bewildered, but once an attack was over, his faculties returned to normal except for a hole in his memory for the time during which he was confused. The prognosis is pretty good in cases such as these. The phenomenon is called transient global amnesia, and people who have it usually have no more than a few recurrences. It may have to do with a temporary chemical or electrical imbalance in the brain or a very small stroke to which the body is able to adjust over a period of time. When such episodes are accompanied by a loss of consciousness, however, the problem is more serious.

Head injuries often produce a concussion of the temporal lobes against the bony base of the skull, which causes a temporary loss of memory called amnesia. Although we often think of amnesia as being rare and quite severe, any strong blow to the skull can bring on a mild form. If you knocked your head against your windshield in an automobile collision, you might find yourself unable to remember where you were going or what you were doing in the several minutes before and after the impact.

Even severe cases of amnesia related to head injury, however, often clear up by themselves. When I was an air force neurosurgeon in Germany, I treated a master sergeant (a former German national) who suffered a very severe brain injury in an accident that resulted in a period of prolonged unconsciousness. When he awoke he was not able to speak at all for seven or eight days. His first words, and his first understanding of words, occurred in his mother tongue, German. When he recovered further, we found that he was able to speak French. Three months passed before he was able to understand any English, and it was almost six months before his comprehension of English returned to normal.

These examples of memory loss are dramatic and extreme. But most often the kind of person who consults me and other neurosurgeons or neurologists is someone over age forty who has some problem in remembering names or even telephone numbers. This is a very common complaint, called benign memory loss. It is not unusual for people of any age to sometimes have difficulty remembering names or even events that are routine or do not have any specific content or emotional charge to them. The loss is benign because it does not get worse and it does not affect mental performance. People tend to notice the condition more when they are under a lot of stress.

Many mental processes contribute to memory besides the encoding of information in the brain, and there are a number of reasons that people may forget even things that seem important to them. The ability to remember is primarily related to forces of attention and distraction. If there is not enough attention and too much distraction, then perfect concentration on an event is impossible. A person's ability to concentrate is often related to how new or different something is.

Suppose you came to see me and I was wearing a bright pink

lab coat. You would probably remember that because the novelty of it would draw your attention. If the lab coat was gray or off-white you might not remember it because it would look typical and other things would distract you.

Besides distraction, depression and panic over the fear of a supposed memory loss can disable the memory process severely. Panic, in fact, can trigger or fuel a depression. It's a terribly vicious cycle. Depression erodes concentration, enhances distraction, and produces an even more severe learning problem for recent memory. If the depression is very severe, the loss of memory may be as profound and disabling as that which occurs in true Alzheimer's disease. Even skilled neurologists may have difficulty differentiating between memory loss owing to true Alzheimer's and the recent memory loss that occurs in what is known as the "pseudodementia" of depression.

DEPRESSION

I believe that the number one cause of memory loss in the elderly is not Alzheimer's or for that matter any other brain disease. It is the completely reversible condition of depression. When younger people get depressed and become forgetful or inattentive, they usually have enough other things going on in their lives to pull them along during the low period. Many elderly, however, lead relatively sedentary lives to begin with. As depression sets in, people around them (usually family members) jump to the conclusion that the memory problems they see are due to brain disease. Suddenly, a parent or grandparent begins to look incapable of handling his or her own affairs. It doesn't take long before a combination of the wrong kind of prescription medication and a deadening hospital stay produce an apparent dementia that requires institutionalization. What triggers the depression in the first place? Usually the death of a spouse or an accident that leaves the person disabled or less mobile than usual.

One such person I discovered was a woman in a nursing home who had been a successful designer and had been married to the same man for fifty-six years. After her husband died, she became quite depressed and agitated and her doctor put her on Haldol to calm her down. The Haldol and the depression left her in a state of semibewilderment such that she could no longer run her own affairs. Her children panicked. They appointed a guardian and had her placed in an expensive nursing home in Connecticut. She stayed there just long enough (under more and different medications) to become diagnosed as "incurably demented," and she was given additional medication to keep her quiet and submissive.

As months went by and she showed no signs of dying, her family decided that a prolonged stay in the nursing home would consume their inheritance, so they stripped her of her assets to make her technically impoverished and eligible for Medicaid. Once that happened, she was transferred to a rather drab nursing home in New England to live out the rest of her life. When I first saw her, she looked just like all the other demented patients there. Unlike them, however, she was able to interpret proverbs quite well. When I discovered that, I had all her medications stopped for a few weeks. Then I found myself talking face to face with a woman who was no more demented than I.

Could her doctor or even her children have discovered, as I did, that she was not demented? Of course they could have, if they had bothered to give her a simple fifteen-minute mental status exam.

UNDERSTANDING LANGUAGE DISORDERS

Besides identifying memory problems, the mental status examination is particularly useful in tracing language problems, which is one of the reasons I feel the exam is so important. So much of what we do is connected in one way or another with language ability. And discovering problems in this area early can lead to better prognoses.

Repeating a phrase such as "No ifs, ands, or buts," naming objects, spelling *world* backward, reading a simple sentence and then writing it from memory, and even obeying commands that require skilled movements test portions of the brain concerned with speech function.

Anatomically, speech is centered in three parts of the brain — Broca's area, Wernicke's area, and part of the temporal lobe. People who have strokes, tumors, or injuries to the anterior one of these three areas (Broca's) lose fluency and have difficulty forming words, and both the quality and quantity of their speech is reduced. While he was president, Dwight Eisenhower had a stroke that affected the speech center of his brain; although he recovered a considerable amount of speaking ability, his speech remained hesitant during the rest of his presidency and throughout his life.

Problems in speaking and communicating can also come about through damage to other areas of the brain, and they produce their own characteristic problems. Strokes, tumors, or injuries in the parietal lobes involving the surface or cortex of the brain produce a lack of understanding, sometimes of both the written word and the spoken word. People who have this kind of abnormality speak fluently, but the content of their speech is very shallow. They are usually unable to understand language and environmental cues that would allow them to enter into a meaningful conversation. If you ask them how they feel, for example, they may respond by saying something like "The grass is greel."

Injuries to the inner surface of the temporal lobe, deep to the ear, can result in difficulty naming objects, such as the clasp of a watchband. And interruptions between the frontal and parietal speech centers produce what is known as a conduction aphasia. Victims of this disorder are fluent, and their ability to understand spoken language is relatively preserved, but repetition of test phrases is difficult, and their speech is full of errors, called paraphasias, in which they use the wrong words or mix words up. One syllable might be correct and the second erroneous, as in "penel" for "pencil."

Language disorders come in many varieties, and different factors can change a person's response to declining abilities. James was seventy-nine years old, but his meticulous grooming, attentive blue eyes, and alert posture made him seem many years younger. He visited me with his wife and son, both of whom appeared sympathetic but resigned. For nine years, James had had a progressive deterioration in his mental abilities, specifically in his speech. As the chief librarian of a major college collection, his whole life had been involved with books and literature. This made it seem all the more tragic to me when I saw him reduced to a few words of interjection and social speech and unable to name even the simplest objects.

The cause of James's problems was a slowly advancing form of Alzheimer's disease. While his friends and family were acutely aware of his language problems, James himself was completely unaware that anything was amiss. People with Alzheimer's rarely complain about problems with language or understanding because the disease destroys not only the brain's language centers but also those parts of the brain that regulate and detect problems with language. When someone *does* complain about decreasing abilities to speak or understand, I suspect that he or she *does not* have Alzheimer's.

James's situation is a good example of the most effective and ideal family response when a loved one gets Alzheimer's. As his condition worsened, his wife and son cared for him at home, the same home he'd lived in for more than forty years, rather than sending him to a nursing home. When he progressively lost his speaking ability, all his other environmental cues stayed the same so that he was able to function, though at a reduced level. If they had taken him out of his familiar environment, he would not have led any sort of normal life. He would have been completely unable to cope. James died in his own home, his dignity intact, and his loving family around him. Clearly, not all Alzheimer's victims are fortunate enough to have the kind of family support James had.

WHAT TO DO IF THERE'S A PROBLEM

If you take a complete mental status examination and make no mistakes, indications are that everything is probably all right. But what should you do if your mental status exam is somehow deficient? The first thing to remember is not to panic. There are a lot of reasons for having a deficient mental status examination that have nothing to do with Alzheimer's disease, strokes, or brain tumors. Indeed, many of the underlying conditions that cause errors on the exam are completely reversible. But you do want to discover what the problem is as quickly as possible and fix it.

In later chapters, we discuss some of the diets, exercises, and other programs you can use on your own to correct mild brain problems. If a problem is obviously severe — with blackouts, fainting spells, fits of uncontrollable temper, or partial paralysis — you should seek medical help, especially to identify reversible brain diseases and to treat them promptly.

What kind of doctor should you look for? You want an experienced and competent physician or psychologist who is thoroughly familiar with brain function and knows how to get to the bottom of a problem quickly. The examinations that are required can be done on an outpatient basis. I emphasize that hospitalization is *not* necessary. Sometimes, neurologists carry out these kinds of examinations; sometimes psychiatrists or psychologists can do a good job. The important thing is that some competent professional *must* carry out the following procedures. If a doctor tells you that he or she doesn't give these tests or doesn't think they are necessary, you should find another doctor. Here are the steps a professional should follow to find out what's wrong.

History

A thorough and complete history, taken by someone who is knowledgeable about brain function, needs to be done first. The clinician should ask questions such as the following: When did the problem start? What are its symptoms? Have you had any previous trouble of this sort? Myriad other questions need to be asked and tabulated. It is often useful for the history taker to talk not only with you but with members of your family and to get records of performance, such as school records or work records, so that he or she can have an objective picture of your history on which to base an opinion.

Physical Exam

A good physical examination, including blood studies, must be carried out. This is the only way to rule out disease of the thyroid, pituitary, adrenals, and pancreas and other diseases that show up in blood tests. Do you have unsuspected diabetes or low blood sugar? Are your nutrition and hydration adequate? Are you anemic? Are your heart and lungs working properly? Is there any source of tiny clots that could break off into your blood vessels and produce transient intellectual problems? Have you had an infectious disease that could have produced a loss of brain function? All of these questions can be answered by a good physical examination.

Psychological Tests

These tests should be of two varieties. The first is called a psychodiagnostic test and includes such things as standard memory tests, intelligence tests, and tests for emotional problems. The other kind of test is a neuropsychological test and is really a quantitative extension of the neurological examination assessing brain function. These tests concentrate on the frontal lobes and executive functions — the ability to plan for the future and the ability to understand the consequences of your behavior. A combination of these two sets of tests is very accurate in detecting a loss of intellectual function. The tests often contain a dementia rating scale, which gives a quantitative rating of how much intellectual function has been lost.

Neurological Exam

If any of the tests so far have uncovered any positive findings, the next step is to get a complete neurological examination by a neurologist. A neurologist not only will repeat a more detailed mental status exam but will also examine the senses — hearing, vision, taste, smell, position sense, touch localization, as well as vibration sense and pin perception. The neurologist will notice any signs of weakness of the facial muscles or the tongue as well as the arms or legs. He or she will look with an ophthalmoscope through the anterior chamber of your eye at the optic nerve head and retina in the back of your eyeball and will also examine your eye movements to be sure that they are smooth and conjugate. He or she will test your visual fields to see if vision to the side, to either right or left, is impaired or constricted. Your coordination and rapid alternating movements will be examined as well as your station, that is, whether you can stand with your feet together and your eyes closed without swaying or falling down. The neurologist will evaluate your ability to walk and hop and will also tap your tendons with a rubber hammer and scratch the soles of your feet.

CAT Scan and MRI

If the neurologist feels it is necessary, two other examinations will be carried out: an x-ray called a computerized axial tomogram, or CAT scan, and magnetic resonance imaging, or MRI. Both give a picture of the structure of the brain, but a CAT scan takes less time and is thus better for anxious people who can't sit still or feel claustrophobic or who have calcified areas that need to be examined with x-rays. Magnetic resonance is better for looking at the back part of the brain and the brainstem and for finding white matter lesions associated with multiple sclerosis.

Brain Wave Tests

If you've had fainting spells or blackouts, brain wave tests also should be done to rule out partial seizures or unusual forms of epilepsy.

I have just described a complete battery of tests that should definitively detect a brain problem if one exists. Other tests could and may be done, but those mentioned here are the major ones. How often does a person who complains of, say, headache problems or a feeling of malaise get the complete battery of tests? Unfortunately, rather seldom.

Usually a doctor reacts to a new symptom by giving the patient just one kind of test. That's what happened to George, a women's clothing buyer, who complained about progressive depression starting about one year before I first saw him. George went to see an internist, who gave him a standard medical examination but no neurological examination or mental status exam.

Two weeks before his first appointment with me, his physician hospitalized him because his depression was getting worse. The doctor started George on antidepressant medication, and within ten days his symptoms showed a slight but definite improvement. Three days later he was discharged. The day after that he was wheeled into my office in a semiconscious state. His CAT scan confirmed the diagnosis: He had an obvious frontal lobe brain tumor that was inoperable.

George could possibly have been saved and successfully treated if the CAT scan had been done six or seven months earlier. While brain tumors occur relatively infrequently, a neurological exam can usually alert a doctor to the possibility, and the diagnosis can be positively made through a CAT scan.

George's physician, a popular internist, was clearly concerned when I called to tell her about George's tumor. Her concern was not only for George but also for herself. She wondered whether George's family would sue her for malpractice and whether, as a defensive practice, she should immediately order CAT scans for all of her other patients who were depressed!

The tragedy of cases like George's is that a complete set of tests taken at the start of a problem, done in one or two days, could save thousands of lives. Yes, such tests can be expensive, but the costs that may be incurred by not doing them, including emergency intervention measures, could be several dozen times greater. I am not advocating that everyone rush out to get the full battery of tests. If you or someone you've tested has no problems on the mental status exam, shows no obvious signs of a deficit, and has no complaints relating to mental functions, there's no reason either to take more tests or to seek medical help.

I haven't written a definitive interpretation of each question on the mental status exam because doing so would literally require an entire book. As I've indicated, poor performance on any given question can be interpreted in a number of ways. That's where an expert, informed opinion can be useful.

If a problem is identified, you will probably have several courses of action to choose from. Whenever possible, it is best to find the cause of the problem rather than to simply ignore the symptoms and hope they will go away.

Sometimes I see people who did not seek treatment right away and I ask them why they waited. They say, "I knew there was something wrong but I thought it would pass." That form of denial is especially unfortunate when a neurological problem persists or gets progressively troublesome.

In some cases nothing can be done, but more often than not some treatment is available and can help. Generally, the sooner treatment starts, the better a person's chances for improvement. It can be difficult to face the fact of a brain disease or injury, but if you suspect any kind of problem, I urge you to have yourself tested. Knowing, one way or the other, can make a big difference in your life.

Chapter 4

Maintaining Brain Power Fitness

Conventional medical wisdom tells us not to smoke, not to drink, not to eat too much (particularly the wrong kinds of foods), and not to take drugs (especially controlled substances). Even though you might think those guidelines for living are well established, they really aren't. Your doctor says, "Make sure you don't eat foods that are bad for you, especially foods with a lot of salt or cholesterol. Salt and cholesterol are bad for you."

Does this mean you should avoid all salt and all salty foods all of the time? And what about the thousands of other foods out there? They don't put labels on eggs saying, "Warning: Contains Cholesterol." How do you know whether eggs are all right to eat?

When doctors advise you about which foods to eat and which to avoid, or which medications to take and not to take, they usually don't consider whether their advice is good for optimal brain function. They assume that if it's good for the heart or digestive system, it must be good for the rest of you. That's not necessarily so.

We look at the brain power diet in Part III, but for now I want to discuss some things your doctor may have advised you to do and explain when it is appropriate to discard medical advice that does not work for you.

ENSURING A GOOD BLOOD SUPPLY

The brain is very susceptible to a decrease in its blood supply, which can cause a stroke. Stroke usually has a sudden onset and is produced by disease of blood vessels in the brain. There are two varieties of stroke. The most common involves the partial or complete plug-up of a blood vessel that brings blood to the brain, resulting in the death of brain tissue irrigated by that blood vessel. In medical jargon the death of brain tissue is called cerebral infarct. The second kind of stroke, which produces a cerebral hemorrhage, involves bleeding into or around the brain. It is commonly associated with blood vessel disease such as atherosclerosis (hardening of the arteries), and it may take place deep within the brain where blood vessels divide. Many people who suffer a brain hemorrhage, particularly in the deeper portions of the brain, experience an immediate paralysis in one arm and leg, a loss of speech, and even unconsciousness. However, this is not always the case.

Laura was a ramrod-straight seventy-eight-year-old matriarch referred to me by a physician who couldn't explain or treat the sudden onset of severe headaches that Laura was experiencing. "I want someone to help me get rid of these headaches," Laura told me. "And I don't see what good it will do to take this special x-ray picture. I don't need x-rays, I need relief."

Both Laura and her physician were amazed that a golf ball–sized brain hemorrhage showed up on her CAT scan. Fortunately, the location of the hemorrhage was toward the surface in an area of the brain that doesn't have anything to do with speech and movement. The hemorrhage caused a deficit that we could test for on neurological examination but that was not immediately obvious to the unskilled observer. Although her hemorrhage was sizable, it did not produce a critical change within the brain, and it did not require surgery.

For some time now, doctors have known that people with high blood pressure have a much greater susceptibility to stroke (especially brain hemorrhage) than people who have normal blood pressure. And the control of high blood pressure, usually with various antihypertensive medicines, has reduced the incidence of stroke. Unfortunately, it occasionally has also produced a new kind of problem that doctors are not as well aware of.

Someone who ought to have known the dangers of antihypertensive medication, but didn't, was a forty-five-year-old emergency room physician named Courtney who came to see me because her memory was failing and she also noticed that she had difficulty walking. Courtney had had clinical hypertension for at least a decade and during that time she had treated the problem with a variety of antihypertensive medicines. My first thought in accounting for her recent symptoms was that she might have had a small stroke, but her CAT scan showed something unusual: a decrease in the density of deep brain tissue in the border zone between two major arteries. I began to wonder if Courtney's antihypertensive therapy was working at all. But repeated checks of her blood pressure showed that it was in the normal to low-normal range and, in fact, when she stood up her blood pressure often dropped into a subnormal range.

Courtney was one of many patients who experience low blood pressure from taking too much antihypertensive medication. The medicine caused her to develop a loss of intellectual function, particularly loss of memory, and she also had some death of brain tissue (infarcts) in the border zone and impending infarcts (small strokes) from loss of deep tissue in her brain. In trying to keep her blood pressure down as she thought she should, Courtney actually overmedicated herself to the point of causing brain damage.

The use of antihypertensive medication is so widespread that low blood pressure, instead of high blood pressure, is becoming a common problem. Unfortunately, many physicians put hypertensive patients on these drugs without changing their diets or reducing the amount of hard fat and cholesterol they take in every day. So even if their blood pressure comes down to the normal or low-normal range, the disease inside their blood vessels, particularly blood vessels to the brain, continues unchecked, with subsequent narrowing of the channels that deliver blood to the brain. Such people become more susceptible to drops in blood pressure. There just isn't enough pressure to ensure adequate irrigation of blood through the blood vessels of the brain.

At times I have found it necessary to increase a person's systemic blood pressure to ensure proper irrigation of vital brain structures. One patient who began to suffer transient episodes of blindness and occasional fainting spells had a constriction in the lumen of a carotid artery, one of the great blood vessels in the neck that carry blood to the brain. Special studies of this man's blood vessels also showed that they had narrowed within the brain itself. Nevertheless, I hoped that removing the constriction in his carotid artery would improve the blood flow to his brain. I surgically repaired the artery and reestablished the blood flow of this major blood vessel on the right side. When the patient woke up from surgery he was able to move his left arm, but two hours later he began to get weakness in that arm and a drooping of the left side of his face. I reexamined his wound and found that it was satisfactory, but his blood pressure was in a low-normal range. So I gave him some medicine to increase his blood pressure, and the function in his left arm and face returned. Eventually, his blood pressure stabilized at a slightly elevated level, which, for him, was essential for adequate circulation in his brain to keep his left arm and face functioning normally.

These examples illustrate that no universal rule should be applied to everyone about keeping blood pressure down. Many mildly hypertensive people can have their blood pressure sufficiently reduced by consuming a low-sodium diet and do not need to take antihypertensive drugs that can depress their blood pressure to dangerous levels. Through diet, it is often possible to keep blood pressure in a normal range in patients who do not have other medical problems, such as kidney disease. We examine diet in detail in Chapters 9 and 10.

OXYGEN SUPPORTS LIFE

Often lost in the health warnings to keep blood pressure down is the fact that your blood pressure can be in a normal range while your brain is starving for oxygen. Oxygen is one of the vital elements carried to the brain in blood, and a number of factors can lower concentrations of it to dangerous levels.

I'm not going to lecture you about the dangers of smoking — by now you should know that smoking causes lung cancer and other harmful side effects. But I want to briefly explain the effect that smoking has on the brain.

Smoking may cause changes in the structure of the lungs that lower oxygen concentrations in the blood. These lowered concentrations can lead to reduced function of brain cells from lack of oxygen. Perhaps because of some genetic factors, nerve cell malfunction related to oxygen starvation isn't equally severe in every smoker, but everyone who has lung problems from smoking experiences it to some extent.

My barber for twenty years had this problem. A lifelong smoker, Jean was constantly fighting for breath. Though he tried to quit smoking, he couldn't, and eventually his chronic oxygen deficit caused his memory and attention to fail. Indeed, it became so difficult for him to concentrate that I sometimes had to stop him as he began to clip the hair on the side of my head he had already cut.

Besides smoking, any medical problems that cause the lungs to become less efficient, such as pneumonia, decrease oxygen levels in the blood. When that happens, it is advisable to increase the oxygen supply artificially to keep oxygen levels in the brain at normal concentrations.

How can you tell if you're running an oxygen deficit? The body's internal mechanism warns you with symptoms such as dizziness and lightheadedness. Only a thorough physical exam and analysis of your blood can determine precisely why dizziness occurs. It is not a trivial symptom, and I strongly urge anyone who feels dizzy and whose lips and fingernails take on a blue cast to get a complete physical. The problem may not be just with the lungs. An associated heart problem in pumping the blood to pick up oxygen in the lungs, or a lack of red blood cells or hemoglobin to transport the oxygen, could also produce similar symptoms.

STOP POISONING YOUR OWN BRAIN

Learning what can poison your brain is as important as learning what will improve brain function. Some members of the medical community tout therapies or drugs they think will make you live longer. Even doctors may misinterpret complex medical data or fail to take into account all the factors. Sometimes, though well intentioned, they say things that are patently false. My favorite doctor-generated myth is the notion that consuming a moderate amount of alcohol each day will make you live longer.

The reasoning behind this fallacy is as follows: It's been demonstrated that a small amount of alcohol in the blood increases the levels of high-density lipoproteins (HDLs). Increased levels of HDLs are related to a decrease in atherosclerosis of blood vessels. Studies indicate that people who drink moderately have a lower incidence of heart attacks and occlusive stroke than people who don't drink at all. Therefore, so the thinking goes, a certain amount of alcohol each day must be good for you. The mechanism for this effect is unknown, however, because the HDL fraction influenced by alcohol is not the one that prevents atherosclerosis. Furthermore, the apparent protective effect is small and may be related to factors other than alcohol consumption.

What the advocates of this theory don't tell you is that while moderate alcohol consumption may reduce the risk of one kind of stroke that results from the shutting down of a blood vessel, incidence of a less frequent stroke, the kind associated with brain hemorrhage, actually increases in patients who take a moderate amount of alcohol. Nevertheless, these arguments about the value of alcohol are really irrelevant for at least two reasons: First, there are better ways of using diet and specific medicines to alter the lipoprotein balance and avoid occlusive blood vessel disease. Not the least of these is the simple remedy of taking a single aspirin or aspirin product every other day. But second and more important, the doctors who talk about the effect of alcohol on the blood vessels or the fat metabolism are overlooking the important physiological point that the chief effect of alcohol on the human body occurs in the brain. Alcohol is a tissue poison: It poisons the brain.

Some doctors deny all this and claim that the diseases of the brain associated with chronic alcoholism are really caused by other factors. They point to the fact that Korsakoff's psychosis, a disease that produces loss of memory in chronic alcoholics, is really caused by a thiamine or vitamin B_1 deficiency. Others claim that the reason alcoholic patients become demented is not that alcohol causes chronic brain poisoning but that alcoholic patients tend to suffer head injuries. This is partially true, but neither of those points explains the brain deterioration that takes place in chronic alcoholics who do not have the vitamin deficiency and who have never experienced a serious head injury.

In 1962, a Canadian brain scientist named J. C. Lee demonstrated the effects of alcohol on the blood-brain barrier in experimental animals. The blood-brain barrier is a natural barrier around the capillaries of blood vessels in the brain that prevents unwanted substances from coming in contact with the delicately balanced neuroelectric and neurochemical environment in many brain cells. This barrier can be upset by various kinds of diseases and is destroyed by brain tumors, strokes, some infections, and for varying periods of time by brain injuries. It is also destroyed, temporarily, by alcohol.

During the period when the brain is poisoned by alcohol, the brain is just as disabled as it would be by a tumor, infection, injury, or stroke. The difference is not in the degree of brain disability produced by alcohol but in the duration of the disability. Strokes and brain tumors are brain insults that last for a long time. Brain injury from alcohol lasts for a relatively short time, from a matter of hours to as long as a day, depending on the amount of alcohol consumed. However, repeated doses of alcohol produce changes in the structure of the brain, remove some of the normal fatty substance around the neurofibers, which causes a shrinkage of the internal structures of the brain, and expand the fluid-filled spaces within the brain. If this brain poisoning hasn't continued for too long, the structural changes in the brain may be reversible.

One night, when I was on call at Boston City Hospital, I treated a young woman who was unconscious because of a head injury that she sustained in an automobile collision. I discovered that her brainstem, the tube of neural tissue that connects the spinal cord to the large brain and contains the center of consciousness, was severely injured. Ironically, the man who drove into her was an off-duty policeman whose blood alcohol level indicated that his brain was profoundly poisoned. Both the policeman and his victim were lying unconscious in the same intensive care unit, and when I tested their levels of consciousness, or rather stupor, there wasn't much difference between them. However, the young woman was the victim of a severe brain injury, whereas the policeman was unconscious because of brain poisoning from alcohol. He would recover, she would not.

I once gave a talk to an airline pilots' organization about the relation of abnormal aggression and brain injury. I spoke about the effects of brain poisons such as cocaine, amphetamines, barbiturates, and angel dust, but the mention of the last item on my list, alcohol, produced an ominous and hostile response from my audience. Later, one of the other speakers, a senior United States senator, paraded in front of the lectern with cocktails in both hands saying, "I've had my share of drinks in my time, and do I look poisoned?" He thought I was joking.

Because many famous people have used alcohol and other drugs and remained productive, it was assumed that the substances had no lasting side effects. I will just point out that brain poisons won't improve your mental performance any more than one would say that temporal lobe epilepsy helped Dostoevski write epic literature. Brain poisons, of whatever stripe and in whatever amount, can only decrease the quality of your life. Don't use them.

BEYOND TRADITIONAL MEDICINE

It is the physician's responsibility to make certain that the regulatory or homeostatic mechanisms are working properly in each patient he or she sees. A blood test can determine if metabolites and electrolytes are present in normal concentrations. The levels of folate and vitamin B_{12} also indicate if you've been receiving enough nutrition and enough vitamins.

It is essential that you consume foods with the necessary vitamin, protein, and energy components and that you are able to chew and digest them so that the deficiency state does not occur. In discussing minimal requirements for vitamins, protein, and energy foods, I'm not talking about the more controversial aspects of nutrition, such as megavitamin therapy or the use of tryptophan, the amino acid that produces the neurotransmitter serotonin. The latter has been advocated for the correction of sleep disorders as well as the treatment of depression.

The bigger question is what happens to our brain when we eat more than the recommended minimum amounts of certain vitamins, minerals, or amino acids. Do they give us supernormal function? And what about amino acids like tyrosine, which is related to the production of norepinephrine and dopamine? Do they increase our alertness and enable us to concentrate more effectively? And what about choline and lecithin? Do increased doses improve our memory? These questions take us beyond the ordinary nutritional advice we receive from our physicians about staying healthy and bring us to the cutting edge of a newly perceived relationship between food intake and behavior.

I discuss these issues in Part III, which is devoted to helping you build and rebuild your brain power. But first let's take a closer look at what you can do to prevent the loss of brain power.

The Prevention of Brain Power Loss

Chapter 5

Alzheimer's Disease, Depression, and Benign Memory Loss

One of my friends, a seventy-year-old retired army officer, called me recently to tell me about a new and important business deal he was involved in. Oscar often calls to discuss business, family, and sports news with me, and there was nothing out of the ordinary in his language or speech to make me think that he had anything wrong with his brain. But I had to admit I was unsettled when I received a call from Oscar twelve hours later in which he repeated precisely the same information about his business deal, using almost precisely the same words. He had no recollection that he had called me before.

Benign memory loss, in which we may forget names or telephone numbers, is not unusual in people over the age of forty-five, and it's not alarming. However, if someone who is not brain-poisoned with alcohol or drugs loses an entire epoch of memory, it is an immediate indicator to begin brain testing.

To put the episode with my friend in a clearer perspective, look at it this way. If my wife sent me to the supermarket to buy five items, it would not be very unusual if I didn't remember one or two. If I were particularly distracted, I might even forget all five. But if I returned home and did not remember that I had even been to the supermarket, my memory loss would be far more serious and might indicate the start of a degenerative brain disease.

The disease that is most often associated with the loss of intellectual and memory functions and that is progressive (it becomes worse over time) is Alzheimer's disease. If it occurs in someone after age sixty, it is usually termed senile dementia of the Alzheimer's type. If it occurs before age fifty-five, it is termed presenile dementia. These age divisions are arbitrary because we are really talking about the same clinical entity.

When my partner, neurologist Tom Sabin, and I started to do surveys of nursing homes in the greater Boston area in the late 1970s, many of the people we saw with dementing illnesses were labeled senile or were described as suffering from hardening of the arteries. We found that more than 90 percent of all the patients in nursing homes had some loss of intellectual function or memory; almost 40 percent had Alzheimer's disease, and another 20 percent were suffering from strokes.

Surprisingly, 20 percent of the patients had a variety of causes for their dementing symptoms, all of which would have been completely treatable had they been given the proper diagnosis. The other 20 percent had a mixture of treatable and untreatable diseases, the combination of which made their symptoms a lot worse than they might have been if the treatable conditions had been corrected.

I was amazed by our findings. For the first time it struck me that tens of thousands of people were being put away prematurely in nursing homes when, in fact, they could have been leading productive lives.

When we published our results in the *Journal of the American Medical Association* in 1982, our conclusions were heralded by the popular press, and families began to tell the doctors who were taking care of their parents what the doctors themselves should have known: Senility is not the natural consequence of aging. If someone's brain isn't working properly, it is because of brain disease or injury.

I'd like to report that our study led to more careful diagnosis and treatment of the elderly, but I know it didn't. What I noticed instead was a change in the way elderly patients were labeled. The diagnosis of hardening of the arteries or senility rapidly fell out of favor. Doctors began labeling the same patients with a more modern diagnosis: Alzheimer's disease, a catchall term that quickly became overused.

In 1950, Sir Alec Guinness starred in a movie called *Last Holiday* in which a careless doctor misdiagnosed a healthy man as having the fictitious Lampington's disease, a supposedly degenerative and fatal illness. I'm afraid that too often the diagnosis of Alzheimer's is handed out as carelessly as the made-up Lampington's disease. Dr. Alois Alzheimer himself would probably be astounded to see how many people today are thought to have his disease, especially since it was virtually unknown before he identified it in 1907. One of my friends, a utilization review nurse, remarked to me in jest that she found so many diagnoses of Alzheimer's in southern Massachusetts hospitals that it must be an infectious disease.

Today, Alzheimer's disease should be a diagnosis of exclusion, that is, it should be given only when everything else has been positively ruled out. We can almost always identify Alzheimer's at postmortem examinations because of characteristic findings in the brains of victims, but an Alzheimer's diagnosis, without adequate testing, gives the impression that the doctor who uses it knows more than he or she really does. Tragically, many patients are consigned to this diagnosis who have treatable problems, and their real maladies remain undiscovered until it is too late to help them.

A recent study at the University of Toronto Sunnybrook Medical Centre reviewed postmortem anatomical studies of patients who, while they were alive, were clinically diagnosed by more than one doctor as having Alzheimer's. Even in this group, more than 14 percent turned out to have something else.

CLASSIFICATION OF DISEASES UNDER THE ALZHEIMER'S BANNER

Many patients diagnosed as having Alzheimer's disease have a life expectancy of from five to seven years, but this is not always the case, as the following story illustrates. A man named Phil, whose brother was a public transportation executive, went to work as a switchman in one of the main rail yards in the New York area. Very slowly and progressively, Phil lost his memory and other intellectual functions, but he doggedly kept going to work and trying to fulfill his obligations. He was protected by his superiors, who thought they were doing his influential brother a favor. But one day his supervisor was ill, and Phil's single-handed, muddled attempts at switching produced a collision between two freight trains.

After the accident, Phil was brought to one of my colleagues for a diagnosis, and all the tests pointed to a progressive loss of memory and intellectual function caused by Alzheimer's.

Phil was given a disability pension and went to live with his sister. He began following a very strict, identical routine every day. He had his meals at the same time, got up and went to bed at the same time, took a walk in the same place and at the same time, rain or shine. My colleague thought that because Phil's symptoms had lasted for three or four years he probably wouldn't survive much longer, but he was wrong. Ten years later, when Phil became suddenly aggressive and uncooperative and required medication, he went back to the same doctor. Nearly fourteen years after his symptoms started, the disease was still progressing very slowly, not at all like the usual case of Alzheimer's disease. Nevertheless, the diagnosis was later confirmed.

There is strong evidence that some cases of Alzheimer's are inherited through a known genetic mechanism, a finding made more readily in the presenile variety. It's hard to spot a genetically inherited cause when a person's Alzheimer's symptoms begin at age eighty-five and the person may no longer have a parent or child who can be tested for possible familial transmission.

Some researchers have suggested that a viral infection of the brain may be implicated in some kinds of Alzheimer's disease. Others have alleged that the disease is related to a failure of metabolism implicating zinc or vitamin E or excessive aluminum in drinking water. These allegations are, as yet, unproved.

At one time it was thought that all patients with Alzheimer's disease had a defect in the neurotransmitter acetylcholine, particularly in the memory circuits of the temporal lobe. Now we know that other neurotransmitters, such as serotonin, dopamine, norepinephrine, and certain neuropeptides, may also be deficient. There is, indeed, a good deal of variation, especially in the early stages of the disease, and there may be quite a difference in the distribution of brain abnormalities from one patient to another.

Because of variations in onset, duration, and severity, it is possible that the clinical and pathological variations just represent the spectrum of problems that are produced by one disease process. However, it is also possible that there are many subtypes or even different kinds of Alzheimer's disease, which may turn out to have different causes and ultimately quite different treatments.

HOW TO TELL THAT SOMEONE HAS ALZHEIMER'S DISEASE

In most Alzheimer victims, a loss of intellectual function and capacity, the typical first symptoms of the disease, usually occur after age fifty, but they can begin at any age. Children with mongolism, for example, exhibit Alzheimer's symptoms in their second decade of life. Studies in both the United States and England have shown that about 5 percent of elderly people suffer from some kind of dementing illness. In the United States about a million and a half people suffer from severe dementia, and an additional three million are afflicted with a mild to moderate loss of intellectual or memory power. A substantial number of these people do have Alzheimer's disease, but because the diagnosis is difficult to make, even for experienced neurologists, it is not possible to know precisely how many people actually have it.

First symptoms vary dramatically among individuals. One diminutive Minneapolis businessman began to have strange behavior at the onset of evening. When darkness came, he walked through his Victorian home, with its mahogany woodwork and multiple-paneled mirrors, enraged at his own reflection and asking his maid, "Who let that ugly stranger in the house?" Eventually all the mirrors had to be covered. As the disease advanced, night brought out even more difficult symptoms, and he required a night nurse because he often got lost when he tried to return to his bed from the bathroom. Such was the state of his confusion that he opened the door to his clothes closet and addressed his suits, saying, "I am P. Merriman Hunnicut, and I seem to be lost. If you're one of my neighbors I wonder if you could direct me to my home."

Amazingly, when the man's driver delivered him to his office during the daytime, he was quite effective working at his desk, making intelligent decisions about the buying and selling of mortgages. Eventually, though, that facade began to crumble.

Charles, a patient of mine, had a different onset to his Alzheimer's syndrome. One night he simply became disoriented when he was driving his car back from the symphony. He had previously traveled a familiar route, but that night he happened to take an unusual turnoff and became completely and hopelessly lost. He finally abandoned his car and flagged down a taxi to get home. Charles never drove after that. As the disease worsened, his world and orientation shrunk so that he required a companion everywhere. Finally, he even had difficulty finding his way from one room to another in a place where he had lived for more than seven years.

In many cases of Alzheimer's, the gradual development of memory loss is the first noticeable major symptom. Vocabulary and word understanding rapidly diminish, and as a consequence an Alzheimer patient will ask a question over and over. On mental status examinations, such a patient will show deficits not only in recent memory (in being able to remember three or four objects for a few minutes) but also in remote memory. Alzheimer victims do poorly on the parts of the mental status exam that deal with mathematical calculations, and they often have great difficulty balancing their own checkbooks. Proverb interpretation, even in early stages of the disease, is usually concrete. That is, a person will interpret the proverb "People in glass houses shouldn't throw stones" as meaning it will break the glass. The person also may have the peculiar tendency to repeat the spoken phrases to him- or herself to make sense of them. Furthermore, the visual-spatial orientation problems that often begin with an inability to orient oneself geographically, as when driving an automobile, may progress to the point where the Alzheimer victim will have difficulty reproducing the simplest geometric patterns when asked to copy them.

I often see Alzheimer patients who are not able to use tools and who are quite incapable of shaving or applying makeup. Complex planning for the day and other executive functions are substantially diminished. Most important, the person has difficulty with language, starting with simply forgetting words, especially proper names and progressing to the point where fluent speech is seriously impaired. The person may interrupt each sentence while he or she pauses to search for the desired word. Even the repetition of words spoken by others, which in the early stages of the disease can be done perfectly, may finally become impossible. Toward the latter stages, incontinence and mutism cause the most serious adjustment problems for those who take care of the afflicted person.

Contrary to popular belief, Alzheimer patients do not become paralyzed, nor do they have sensory loss or a loss of vision or hearing. If these symptoms occur, it is because either the diagnosis of Alzheimer's is incorrect or the disease has been complicated by another disease of the brain such as a stroke.

HOW TO TELL THAT SOMEONE DOES NOT HAVE ALZHEIMER'S DISEASE

Most of the people who come to my office complaining of memory loss have either a depression or are brain-poisoned from overmedication with heart pills or psychiatric drugs. The very fact that they can and do give me detailed and rather elaborate complaints about their memory loss or difficulty in thinking is in sharp distinction to the patients with true Alzheimer's disease, who usually have few complaints or concern about a loss of memory. Furthermore, the amount of self-education and worry they've gone through contrasts markedly with Alzheimer patients, who are usually unconcerned about their problem.

Some people consult me because other members of their family, usually a parent, have had some kind of dementing illness, and they're afraid that as they approach midlife they are getting the same kind of disorder. It always surprises me to see people in their thirties concerned about memory loss to such an extent that they become depressed. It is in fact their depression that fuels their loss of attention and their difficulty with memory.

What, then, is the easiest way to tell if you *don't* have Alzheimer's disease? A simple mental status exam is what I recommend. Alzheimer patients usually have a consistently reduced ability to perform many of the tests, while those who are depressed (whom we sometimes call pseudodementia patients when their loss of brain power is caused by a depression and not brain disease) have rather excellent preserved intellectual abilities. Their performance on the mental status exam may be uneven; for example, they may be able to interpret proverbs quite well or give a very cogent history of what has been happening to them in the past few days. At the same time, they may get zero out of three items right on a test of recent memory. Such test results are a telltale sign of depression, not Alzheimer's.

I have seen twenty people who are anxious or depressed and who complain of memory loss for each person who has a true dementing illness. However, in the early stages of Alzheimer's disease a few people may also be agitated and depressed, worsening their symptoms. Some elderly people with pseudodementia outwardly resemble Alzheimer patients almost precisely. Distinguishing between the two can often be difficult, even for an experienced neurologist. Tests such as CAT scans also may not be able to differentiate between them because a seventy- or seventy-five-year-old with normal brain function may have a substantial reduction of brain volume on the scan.

Some elderly and depressed patients do not respond to psychotherapy or medication (such as antidepressant medication) and have been assumed to have a true dementia. For them, one treatment of last resort has sometimes proved effective. The use of small amounts of electroconvulsive (shock) therapy has brought some of these people out of their depressed stupor back to an amazing degree of intellectual function.

I don't recommend electroconvulsive therapy except in the most severe cases for which all conventional therapies have been tried and have failed. It is a risky and little-understood procedure, and I would advise anyone considering it to get at least one other medical opinion before proceeding.

DEPRESSION: SOME DEFINITIONS

Sometimes a head injury can bring on a depression but the diagnosis is missed because of a complicated medical history. That's what happened to Harold, a forty-seven-year-old construction worker who was hit in the head by a freely swinging cable. The blow was delivered to his occipital region (the back of his head), and as he lost consciousness and started to fall, one of his co-workers noticed that his body was twitching. He dropped about five feet and was partially caught, and he soon regained consciousness. He was taken to a local hospital and released when the staff could find nothing wrong. Later, Harold noticed vague headaches accompanied by a gradual and unusual change in his personality.

Previously he'd been a rather happy-go-lucky man who never thought much about the future and who sang and played the guitar to amuse his family. Following the accident, his personality changed. His face continually took on a sad and concerned expression, and he talked a lot about his health. His previously calm approach to life was replaced by an agitated concern over every matter. More alarming to him was that he had difficulty remembering names, places, and dates and spent increasing amounts of his time secluded and staring into space. These changes in personality continued for months and eventually years.

I saw Harold five years after his head injury. While he did poorly on the mental status exam, there was no indication that he had lost brain tissue or that he was having seizures. He tried several times to go back to work, but he seemed confused about doing jobs that he had previously accomplished with little difficulty. Many mornings he didn't have the energy to get up and leave the house. He was puzzled when he awoke at four or five in the morning filled with vague, formless fears and anxieties.

Harold's doctors tried to differentiate between a disabling brain injury related to his accident and an unrelated case of Alzheimer's disease. Certainly his memory loss and deterioration of intellectual abilities were severe enough to fit either category. My testing and examinations led me to believe that he was suffering from a severe depression and that his loss of intellectual and memory abilities came under the heading of pseudodementia secondary to his depression. Counseling and psychotherapy didn't reverse his problem, but a specific antidepressant medication produced a dramatic and beneficial change after three weeks of therapy.

Everyone experiences periods of sadness and depression. Usually they are mild and self-limited. But specific biochemical changes in the brain can produce prolonged and severe depression in some people.

When you hear the word *depression,* you usually think of someone who has slowed down, is sad, perhaps crying, and apathetic. But in truth many people who are depressed merely become anxious and agitated. When they bring these symptoms to their doctors, they are often treated with drugs like Ativan and Valium to make them feel more relaxed. Unfortunately, those kinds of medications only make the depression worse.

Neuropsychological and psychodiagnostic tests of people with depression often show them to be hyperdistractible with short attention spans. Their reduced attention and concentration abilities lead directly to poor performance and complaints of deficient memory. Because of their lack of concentration, they do not acquire new memories. Finally, with the retardation resulting from depressed brain function, they even have trouble retrieving old memories.

Almost every person who tests positive for severe depression has an element of pseudodementia, regardless of how old he or she is. However, when depression occurs in the elderly, particularly those in nursing homes, its victims take on all the outward signs and symptoms of Alzheimer's disease, and it can be extremely difficult to tell the two conditions apart. That's why depression and the pseudodementia that it produces are called the great impersonator of Alzheimer's disease.

I can't emphasize enough how important it is to differentiate between the two. Depression is a completely treatable entity, whereas Alzheimer's, for now at least, is not. If I have any doubt when I am diagnosing someone, I always try an antidepressant regimen. That, it seems to me, ought to be standard medical practice.

WHAT TO DO ABOUT DEPRESSION

The most important thing to keep in mind about depression is that some people, either because of familial tendencies or biochemical disturbances, are more likely to get a severe depression and are less able to recover from it than others. Also, depression can hit at any time, and it often masquerades as some other disease, such as a dementing illness.

One way to prevent depression is to maintain good brain nutrition — avoid brain poisons such as alcohol and cocaine and make certain that the environment surrounding the brain cells is provided with the essential vitamins, nutrients, and oxygen levels. Another important defense against depression is the acquisition of brain-focusing skills that allow you to relax brain function and sharpen certain abilities so they operate at effective levels in helping to control your environment. Both of these programs — the assurance of adequate brain nutrition on the one hand and the brain exercise program on the other — are taken up in the next section.

States of sadness, boredom, fatigue, and frustration and even mild depression are perfectly normal reactions to our sometimes hostile environment. However, these responses should not lead to clinical depression or require you to consult a physician, psychologist, or psychotherapist. They should stimulate you to take stock of your environment and see what you can do to change it.

Clinical or endogenous depression, however, is not just a sad response to life adjustment problems, and it can develop into a very serious brain disease, often with concomitant agitation. If endogenous depression becomes symptomatic, medical assistance is mandatory. A competent assessment should be carried out by a psychiatrist or other physician to determine the risk of suicide and the immediate steps that should be taken to prevent it.

Professional psychotherapists have had some success in relieving the less severe forms of depression. More important, the medical profession has developed a variety of antidepressant drugs that are dramatically effective in reversing many severe cases. The specialists who administer these drugs are often called psychopharmacologists.

What happens when drug therapy fails? It did fail for Jenna, a seventy-two-year-old with severe behavioral problems whom I saw in a hospital for the elderly. She had been lying in bed, mute and unresponsive to questions, for about four and a half weeks. All our tests failed to confirm either strokes or Alzheimer's disease. Jenna received the full gamut of antidepressant medication with no apparent benefit. Her physicians told me they were going to give her electroconvulsive therapy, and they wanted to know whether there was any brain contraindication to proceeding. Given her history and the severity of her illness, I saw no reason why it should not be tried as a last resort.

Remarkably, five weeks later I met Jenna walking around the halls of the hospital. Her recovery was nothing short of remarkable. She didn't remember my earlier visit, but her speech content was almost normal and she seemed bright and alert. Shortly afterward she was discharged to her own apartment, where she lived with a married daughter. I never thought electroconvulsive therapy would work on someone who was mute and seemed to have severe brain disease on examination. But because I have seen it work, you should be aware of it as an option of last resort in severe cases.

WHAT TO DO ABOUT ALZHEIMER'S DISEASE

First the bad news. Right now there isn't a lot that doctors can do for people who really do have Alzheimer's disease. More encouraging, however, is that other diseases of the brain can occur at the same time and can make the symptoms of Alzheimer's much worse. Depression is one of those symptoms. When the associated depression is adequately treated, the victim's disability is substantially reduced.

In our nursing home survey, as I mentioned, Tom Sabin and I found that 20 percent of the patients with Alzheimer's disease had complicating factors (such as depression) that made their symptoms worse. Effective treatment of those other factors can make a substantial difference to the patient; often, for instance, it allows him or her to live at home instead of in a nursing home.

Another potential complication with Alzheimer's is that people with the disease may develop vitamin and nutritional deficiencies, especially if their eating is unsupervised. These deficiencies also make the symptoms of brain dysfunction worse. The diet of Alzheimer patients should be supplemented with the necessary amounts of vitamins, minerals, and other nutrients to keep their brains working as well as they possibly can. People with brain impairments are more susceptible than the average person to performance changes caused by poor nutrition and electrolyte and fluid imbalances.

In spite of promising leads with the use of vitamin and mineral supplements, we have not yet developed effective therapies for the degenerative brain disease itself.* But we have a number of ways to improve the quality of life for those with Alzheimer's. Chief among them is the institution of a routine that might seem boring or monotonous to us but that really does help such people function better. Alzheimer patients should do the same things at the same time and in the same place day after day. They should have as many memory aids around them as possible, such as a clock or a calendar with the date prominently displayed. Periods of exercise and meals should always be at the same time.

*The one exception might be the prolonged treatment with drugs that enhance acetylcholine in the memory circuits of the brain. Preliminary studies after a year of therapy show encouraging signs for improved memory function.

Alzheimer patients, as well as many elderly people in general, do poorly when they are removed from the home they've always known and placed in new surroundings. This can be true even when they're taken from a familiar room in a nursing home and moved to a different one. Studies carried out under the direction of social scientists at Brandeis University showed that elderly people transferred from one nursing home to another or even from one room in a nursing home to another had an increased incidence of medical complications and a higher rate of death.

Sometimes, in spite of the untoward results, elderly people have to be moved for overriding medical or social reasons. When this happens we should do everything we can to maintain the person's familiar routine.

Remember that a diagnosis of Alzheimer's disease is very difficult to make with 100 percent accuracy. Even the newer radioactive brain scans, using positron emission tomography (PET), do not always differentiate between Alzheimer's disease and other brain problems. If someone you know has been given this label and, based on your own or someone else's observations, you think there's a chance that it is wrong, your first step should be to have the person tested by a qualified neurological professional. There's nothing more tragic than finding someone who was misdiagnosed as having Alzheimer's and who, as a result, was robbed of the final and best years of life.

FREQUENTLY ASKED QUESTIONS

QUESTION: How do Alzheimer's disease and depression fit into the spectrum of diseases that cause people to lose brain function?

ANSWER: Both Alzheimer's and depression are among the most important causes of intellectual and memory loss, especially among the elderly. Alzheimer's disease accounted for about 40 percent of the dementing illness in the nursing home residents

Tom Sabin and I examined. Our subjects were generally people with more severe cases of intellectual and memory loss. Severe depression, also called the pseudodementia of depression, may account for 10 to 15 percent of such cases in a nursing home population. However, outside of the nursing home, in less severe cases, depression is a much more frequent cause of intellectual loss than is Alzheimer's.

QUESTION: Between Alzheimer's and severe depression, which produces the greater deficit?
ANSWER: This may come as a surprise to some people, but the pseudodementia of depression can cause just as much disability as Alzheimer's disease. Even a skilled neurologist can have difficulty differentiating between the two. In both instances, exacerbating features such as poor diet and vitamin deficiency or inadequate fluid intake with an electrolyte or fluid imbalance may be present. Also, some people with Alzheimer's can have a depression that makes the symptoms of their dementing illness much more intense.

The critical difference between Alzheimer's and depression is that depression is almost always treatable and at least temporarily curable. This is not the case with Alzheimer's. But since people with Alzheimer's may have a complicating problem of depression it has been my practice to give these patients a trial of antidepressant medication. A component of their disabling symptoms often disappears, sometimes for months or even a year or two until the disease process advances.

QUESTION: Should a second opinion or neurological evaluation be done when someone has symptoms of intellectual or memory loss? And where does one go to get the right evaluation?
ANSWER: Whether a second evaluation should be done depends on the severity of the memory or intellectual loss. If the loss is trivial, such as difficulty recalling names, it is not necessary to get a complete evaluation. However, if the loss is severe enough

to interfere with activities of daily living, business, or social interactions, then an evaluation by a biologically oriented psychiatrist, a neurologist who is interested in behavioral neurology and Alzheimer's disease, or even a diagnostic psychologist could be helpful.

The place to start is with your family doctor or internist. Ask him or her to refer you to appropriate professional help. Many communities have an Alzheimer and Related Disease Association, which has a list of specialists who are capable of doing the appropriate examinations.

QUESTION: What are the possible benefits of a second opinion?
ANSWER: The most important benefit is the accurate diagnosis of the cause of memory or intellectual loss. In many instances an accurate diagnosis will lead to specific treatment and a reversal of symptoms. If the diagnosis includes loss of brain tissue, such as caused by repeated small strokes, some kind of medical treatment might be feasible to stop the progression of the illness. Even if the diagnosis turns out to be Alzheimer's disease, it should be possible to initiate supportive treatment and lessen the impact of the disease on both the patient and his or her family.

QUESTION: What community services are available to help people who are losing brain function as a result of Alzheimer's?
ANSWER: Almost every large community, and certainly every state, has a chapter of the Alzheimer and Related Disease Association. The association has people staffing telephones with lists of doctors who specialize in the diagnosis and treatment of dementing illnesses. It also has lists of outpatient services and day care centers that are specially suited to treating the victims of Alzheimer's. And many centers will be able to tell you how to contact a visiting nurse association and provide you with a list of community services.

For the less severely afflicted, both community-supported and private day care centers offer a safe environment with strong social programs where working children of Alzheimer victims can leave their parents.

Sometimes the visiting nurse association may be able to provide housekeepers, home health care workers, or companions during the daytime when day care centers are not available or appropriate.

QUESTION: If you suspect that your doctor's diagnosis of Alzheimer's is more a label than a medical fact, what should you do?

ANSWER: You should get a second opinion. If your doctor is unwilling to give you the name of an Alzheimer's specialist, contacting the Alzheimer and Related Disease Association in your community is the appropriate next step. Even though Alzheimer's is a diagnosis of exclusion, a doctor should be able to do enough of the special examinations described in this book to be reasonably sure that the diagnosis is based on good medical evidence.

Making the correct diagnosis requires more than just observation of the person with suspected intellectual or memory loss. Severely disturbed patients may have some other diagnosis besides Alzheimer's to account for their disability. The Alzheimer's diagnosis should not be made by guess or just by a CAT scan of the brain or any other single test. The correct diagnosis requires that all of the tests described in Chapter 4 be performed and that a competent physician review the results and summarize their implications in an integrated clinical report.

Chapter 6

Brain Poisons

Any chemical substances that, when taken into the body in sufficient quantity, alter brain function are potential brain poisons. Does that mean they're necessarily bad? Certainly not. At times, chemical substances are given to people whose brain function is already abnormal, and the chemical alters the abnormality in such a way that the person gets better. However, if the dosage of the chemical were increased to a high enough level, it would cease to have the desired therapeutic effect.

Chemicals of all kinds that do not occur naturally in the brain and that have an effect on brain function are potentially poisonous. The degree of poisoning is related to the amount and concentration of the chemical consumed. When you disturb brain function, you decrease your ability to control your environment, either by cutting yourself off from reality or by changing the way you behave and think. Depending on the poison used, the duration of the poisoning, and the concentration of the poison, the results are either reversible, partially reversible, or permanent. This, in turn, depends on whether, what kind, and how many brain cells are injured or destroyed. Other factors such as age and genetic susceptibility may play a role.

I'm going to tell you about the kinds of substances that I, as a neurosurgeon, find hazardous to the brain. You will recognize some of these substances as being dangerous; others you will not. Surprisingly, even a drug like aspirin, which is universally accepted as being safe, *can* be poisonous to brain cells if a large enough dose is taken. For our purposes, however, we'll look at drugs that are dangerous in relatively small doses and that are likely to affect behavior.

LICIT AND ILLICIT BRAIN POISONS

The major classes of brain poisons, including the opiates, the depressants, the stimulants, and the hallucinogens, all poison various portions of the emotional, or limbic, brain. Other portions of the brain are poisoned as well, but the major effect, and the reason that these drugs are abused, is that they produce hallucinations, euphoria, or a curtain of oblivion that separates the mind from the real world.

Most of these drugs at one time or another were prescribed by physicians as treatment for common complaints. Indeed, opium has been used in medical practice for four thousand years. The abuse of the drug and its incorporation into tobacco enslaved the Chinese empire for centuries in a chronic epidemic of opium brain poisoning.

The discovery of morphine and the hypodermic syringe, which were used during the Civil War, resulted in the spread of a new addiction into the United States. Strangely, morphine was first thought to be a drug that would cure opium addiction. Later, at the beginning of the twentieth century, a cure for morphine addiction was thought to be embodied in the drug heroin, so named because it was supposed to be a "heroic" treatment for morphine addiction.

The physical dependencies that mind-altering drugs produce have been misunderstood or unappreciated by some doctors for decades, and that ignorance continues today. Among the most recent oracles to promulgate false information about narcotics was a Harvard psychiatrist who, in the early 1980s, claimed that cocaine was a relatively safe, nonaddicting euphoriant. Convinced that the drug really was safe, millions of people tried it.

A report by Gawin and Ellingwood from the Yale University Medical School estimated that three million people in the United States abuse cocaine regularly — more than five times the number of heroin addicts. By 1986, almost 15 percent of people in the United States had tried cocaine, many of them twenty-five to thirty-five years old. Recently, however, the median age of first users dropped dramatically, and the number of cocaine-related deaths in the United States increased to more than five per thousand.

Typical of the cocaine abusers I see in my practice are men like Tom, a burly thirty-nine-year-old mechanical engineer who was sent to see me by a court because he was facing charges of attempted murder. A cocaine dealer had coerced Tom's girlfriend into experimenting with the drug, and Tom retaliated by trying to beat the dealer's head with a baseball bat. When he came for testing, Tom had been a cocaine addict for years and often indulged in prolonged periods of cocaine intoxication. The court wanted to know if his brain had been altered by cocaine poisoning.

When I did a computerized electroencephalogram (EEG) and brain map on him, his "signature" corresponded to the brain map evident in a number of other confirmed cocaine addicts. In spite of statements that have appeared in the press claiming that cocaine is nonaddicting, Tom experienced all of the symptoms of a physical addiction, including the crash. After a binge he had an intense depression associated with agitation and anxiety, followed by extreme exhaustion. A craving for cocaine was finally supplanted by a craving for sleep. This was followed by a period of intense eating. These symptoms were repeated each time he indulged in heavy cocaine use and withdrew.

After taking cocaine intermittently for two years, Tom had a series of generalized seizures, or epileptic convulsions. When he recovered from these he decided he was going to stop for good, but when he stopped he found that he had no energy and his interest in his business diminished to the point where he was no longer in control of his own affairs. He also found that he was unable to experience pleasure. These symptoms, which were mild at first, increased in intensity for two or three days and lasted for almost five months after his drug use had stopped completely.

Once Tom no longer had the strong drug craving, he thought that he was home free — that he had licked his cocaine addiction. But he was unaware of a third phase of withdrawal called extinction. This phase consists of periods of strong drug craving brought about by cues such as certain people and places or even the use of alcohol. These cravings can occur months or years after the last use of the drug.

As a result of Tom's cocaine addiction, his mood changed and his new paranoid personality irritated a number of people with whom he had to get along to be a successful businessman. Furthermore, his ability to concentrate and to avoid distractions was sharply reduced. This lack of attention affected his memory and his ability to function not only socially but also in business.

In a way he was fortunate that the first ominous signs of cocaine brain poisoning were the series of epileptic convulsions, because they frightened him enough to make him discontinue using the drug. Tom also avoided one other serious side effect of cocaine brain poisoning — a stroke. A brain infarction or hemorrhage can occur with even a single use of cocaine in a sensitive person. While many deaths from cocaine poisoning are caused by the toxic effects on the heart, brain poisoning is a real and frequent cause of disability. Brain poisoning probably played a major role in Tom's physical attack on the drug dealer. In fact,

the term "dope fiend," which some people think describes heroin abusers, was probably first used to describe cocaine addicts
because of their tendency to commit violent acts.

Aside from its ability to stimulate electrical seizures in the
emotional brain, cocaine also enhances the neurotransmitter
dopamine, which may correlate with unpleasant personality
changes. Other synthetic stimulants, such as the amphetamines,
do precisely the same thing. These brain poisons, usually called
"speed," at one time formed an important component of diet
pills and are dangerous brain poisons whose chronic use not
only generates a loss of intellectual and memory capacity but
also often produces personality changes with outbursts of para-
noia and aggression. Their potential as addicting brain poisons
has frequently been overlooked.

Stimulants such as amphetamines are sometimes altered chem-
ically by drug dealers to make street drugs that produce hallucinations and that poison the inner surface of the temporal lobe
of the brain. These include a methyl amphetamine called STP,
angel dust or PCP, and a methylene amphetamine called MDA.
They're also called "designer drugs" because they can be tai-
lored to poison the brain in such a way that both stimulant and
hallucinogenic effects are produced by the same agent. Marijuana and LSD are also brain poisons that fall into the category
of hallucinogens that alter the perception of time, generate hallucinations, and free their victims from a sense of reality.

Most people are now familiar with drugs that poison the
brain by depressing brain activity — drugs such as chlorohy-
drate, paraldehyde, and especially the various barbiturates. Up
to 1936, before the discovery of Dilantin, an anticonvulsive
drug, phenobarbital was the most effective drug for the treatment of epilepsy. It did reduce the tendency to have seizures, but
it also produced a marked sedative effect and, unfortunately, it
is very habit-forming, as are most of the drugs that produce
sleep.

What is probably not so well known, however, is that the

abrupt withdrawal of sedatives and hypnotics like phenobarbital and the shorter-acting barbiturates can actually precipitate an epileptic seizure in someone who has not previously had one. And, of course, sedatives of all kinds depress brain function and decrease intellectual ability and memory.

ALCOHOL: THE SOCIAL DRUG

Ethyl alcohol is the most frequently used brain depressant; it is also a potent brain poison. Most often we think of alcohol as a stimulant because many people become noisy and hyperactive in the initial stages of alcoholic brain poisoning. However, the euphoriant effects of alcohol are really the result of a depression or poisoning of the executive and inhibiting centers of the brain. As the level of alcohol in the blood rises, brain function is more generally depressed, and the result is sleepiness and even stupor.

One night many years ago, when I was serving as the chief of neurosurgery and also doubling as the chief of neurology at the Air Force Medical Treatment Center in Wiesbaden, West Germany, I was called into the hospital to see a Master Sergeant Jones who was in deep coma. The physician on call was an internist who diagnosed Jones as having had a massive stroke.

When I saw the master sergeant he was comatose — profoundly unconscious, not responding to painful stimuli, with almost no deep tendon reflexes and very slow respirations. His blood pressure was also depressed.

This was long before the invention of CAT scans, so we had no way to determine the immediate presence of a massive hemorrhage in his brain. However, a spinal puncture showed clear spinal fluid, and a blood alcohol level eventually showed a concentration of 55 milligrams per milliliter, an extremely high concentration. I reasoned that if this man had had a stroke there wasn't much we could do for him, but that if he was suffering from severe alcohol brain poisoning we might be able to save his life.

We removed all the unabsorbed alcohol in his stomach through a large stomach tube, and we put an airway in his mouth to be sure that he didn't choke on his secretions. We also gave him a small amount of glucose, vitamin B_1, and some sodium bicarbonate intravenously.

Some patients will die with this degree of alcohol poisoning of the brain. I don't know whether it was because of our treatment or because the patient had a strong constitution, but Jones managed to survive. Not only that, in three days he was discharged from the hospital.

A little later, the doctor who had first seen him approached me in a rather embarrassed way, concerned because he had misdiagnosed the master sergeant as having had a stroke. He, like many other people at that time, just didn't realize what a potent brain poison ordinary ethyl alcohol is. I told him that there was nothing to be ashamed of because alcohol could produce as much brain damage as a stroke, tumor, injury, or infection of the brain. It wasn't the degree of disability that differed, it was the duration. When the brain poisoning subsides, the patient recovers, not quite as well as he or she was before but not as disabled as would be the case with a brain disease or an injury.

Another reason that my medical colleague was concerned about the degree of stupor produced in the master sergeant may have been that he and other career officers had reputations for alcoholic drinking sprees. Even as a physician, he didn't seem to understand that such behavior could actually cause his death. In fact, if our master sergeant had had a slightly higher level of alcohol in his blood, we might not have been able to save him.

Poisoning by alcohol is the most common form of brain poisoning in our society. Delbanco and Barnes of Harvard Medical School report that nearly 10 percent of the population are victims of alcohol abuse. Not only does alcohol produce dramatic changes in behavior, but suicide is thirty times more common among alcohol abusers than it is in the general population. More than half the drivers involved in fatal automobile collisions are brain-poisoned with alcohol, and two-thirds of all adult drowning victims and half of those who die from falls or are burned to death in fires have high blood alcohol levels. According to Delbanco and Barnes, brain and liver poisoning with alcohol is a factor in more than 10 percent of all deaths in the United States, about 200,000 per year. Alcohol-related brain poisoning is also a substantial factor in domestic violence and, like cocaine, plays an important role in violent criminal activities.

I'd like to relate one other case history about alcohol use that is relevant to brain poisoning with alcohol. Harry was a twenty-seven-year-old man who was recently admitted to the Boston City Hospital neurology ward because of uncontrolled epileptic seizures. Before he was admitted, he had been drinking Thunderbird wine persistently for about two and a half weeks, but he finally had to stop because he ran out of money and couldn't get a drink from any of his friends. It wasn't his first time in the hospital. He had been admitted before with exactly the same story: a week or two of spree drinking and then abstinence followed by a series of epileptic seizures.

Harry had been given anti-epileptic medication, but during his drinking spells he forgot to take it or lost it. There was no indication that he ever had epilepsy before he started to drink or that anyone in his family had suffered from epileptic convulsions. None of those things were necessary to produce convulsions or seizures in him or in anyone. Some people, if they drink and absorb enough alcohol and then stop suddenly, regardless of whether they have ever had a drink before, will have epileptic seizures. The only thing that differs between individuals is the amount of alcohol necessary to produce this effect.

Harry was a chronic alcohol abuser, and when the seizures stopped, he eventually went through delirium tremens, in which he saw blue elephants and green snakes and ran a high fever. When we looked at his brain using a CAT scan, we found some shrinkage in the center and expansion of the fluid-filled spaces of the brain, called the ventricles. He also had shrinkage of the back part of his brain, the cerebellum. This loss of brain substance is often seen in long-term alcohol abusers and is a bad prognostic sign for the person who won't stop drinking alcohol.

Incidentally, the characteristics I describe don't occur only in alcoholic derelicts admitted to inner-city hospitals. We noticed the same findings in the brains of a large group of clergymen who abused alcohol and who were being diagnosed at our laboratory with the use of CAT scans. Fortunately, if we can get alcohol abusers to stop drinking, some of the brain changes that we see on CAT scans can be reversed, but only in the early stages of the disorder.

Under ordinary circumstances, brain cells are protected by a physical and chemical blood-brain barrier surrounding the brain capillaries. This barrier acts to keep harmful substances in the blood from penetrating the brain, but the barrier can be broken by tumors, infection, and injuries. It is also broken by even small amounts of ingested alcohol, especially in the limbic or emotional brain, for the duration of the poisoning.

BRAIN POISONS THAT YOUR DOCTOR PRESCRIBES

Angelina was a sixty-eight-year-old Italian woman with a long history of recurrent and severe depressions. Her first bout came on shortly after the birth of her first child and recurred after she gave birth to each of her seven other children. With every ensuing depression, her symptoms seemed to get worse, and it wasn't appreciated at the time that her problem was related to changes in her sex hormone levels. She had received a variety of antidepressant medications and electroshock therapy on at least two occasions, to no lasting effect.

When she came to me, her most recent episode of depression had occurred following the death of her husband. Her doctor had put her on a drug called Elavil, which did in fact improve some of the symptoms of her depression. But after a few weeks of the medication she experienced increasing difficulty with her memory and in carrying out the independent activities of daily living.

In fact, Angelina was referred to me as a candidate for admittance to a nursing home. After I reviewed her case in detail, I noted that she was on high doses of Elavil, a drug that alters brain function. Since she did have abnormal brain function resulting in depression, it was perfectly reasonable for her doctor to give her an antidepressant. But the antidepressant he prescribed had another action that interfered with the neurotransmitter acetylcholine.

Drugs that have that effect, particularly in people over the age of sixty, may have a tendency to alter brain function and bring on signs of dementia. When I took Angelina off the Elavil and substituted another antidepressant that did not interfere to the same degree with acetylcholine transmission in her brain, she was able to get the full antidepressant effect without the complication of memory loss and intellectual deterioration, and she improved substantially.

Sleeping pills and tranquilizers such as Valium and Ativan are quite capable of producing memory loss and intellectual deterioration. Other psychiatric drugs, such as Melaril, lithium, Thorazine, and Haldol, can also interrupt and disturb normal brain function, as was illustrated by the case of Francine, a sixty-two-year-old grandmother who was institutionalized in a nursing home for seventeen months with the diagnosis of Alzheimer's disease. The first thing I noticed in looking at her records was that she was on twenty-seven *different* psychiatric drugs, including sedatives, hypnotics, antipsychotics, and antidepressants — all at the same time! One doctor after another added a medication to see if he could relieve her symptoms without removing any of the previous medications. The result was that her mental symptoms and intellectual deterioration continued to advance and become more severe.

This is an egregious example of what we call "poly-pharmacy," use of multiple drugs that poison a person's brain. I had to be very careful in Francine's treatment because withdrawing the drugs too quickly and altogether could have precipitated severe mental symptoms and a physical withdrawal effect. It took four and a half weeks to gradually wean her from the variety of medications. Amazingly, when we did that, her symptoms of Alzheimer's disease completely disappeared. She was simply the victim of brain poisoning.

Certain combinations of drugs — Melaril and lithium, Haldol and the antihypertensive drug methyldopyl — are particularly likely to produce intellectual deterioration or even an acute confusional state. This happened to Bridgette, a seventy-two-year-old native of Dublin who immigrated to the Boston area in 1960 and worked as a nurse's aide in several hospitals. She developed symptoms that were interpreted as an agitated depression and was put on Melaril and lithium. She became increasingly confused and agitated because she heard voices and saw birds flying over her bed.

After months of taking these medications, toxic levels in her bloodstream built up, and she became drowsy and had periods of stupor. I was called to see her to rule out a blood clot on the brain. Her tests were all negative and I suspected brain poisoning; my recommendation was that her doctors get immediate blood levels of the drugs she was taking and begin a gradual and steady reduction in her medications. Simply discontinuing her medications restored her intellectual abilities.

Some major tranquilizers or antipsychotic medicines, such as Thorazine, Stelazine, and Haldol, poison the brain over a period of time. They also produce a peculiar movement abnormality, called tardive dyskinesia, that can take such forms as involuntary chewing movements or a high-stepping gait called the "peacock walk." Even when the drugs are stopped, the movement abnormalities persist. Recently, therapeutic doses of vitamin E or lecithin have been found to successfully treat some of these symptoms.

A number of medicines that are not necessarily used to treat the brain may have an adverse effect on brain function, particularly in people over age sixty. These include such unlikely medications as eye drops that treat glaucoma (Timoptic and pilocarpine); painkillers such as Darvon; anti–Parkinson's disease drugs such as L-dopa and Symmetrel; heart and blood pressure medications such as digitalis, Inderal, and reserpine; anti-asthma agents such as aminophylline; and gastric drugs such as cimetidine. Table 1 summarizes the classes of prescription drugs that can cause mental changes.

Some elderly individuals are much more sensitive to these general medical agents as they grow older, so that quantities of medicine that didn't hurt them a year or two before suddenly become toxic for their brains. A sixty-eight-year-old former school principal named John, who had retired to a small farm in Virginia, fell into this trap. He was in the habit of taking antihistamines in the late spring for his allergies. One spring his wife was quite alarmed to note that he developed increasing memory loss, which she called forgetfulness, with more frequent periods of

---

Table 1

CLASSES OF POTENTIALLY TOXIC OR
POISONOUS PRESCRIPTION DRUGS

Psychiatric Drugs	*Drugs Used in General Medicine*
Barbiturates	Digitalis preparations
Bromides	Analgesics
Benzodiazepams	Antihypertensives
Phenothiazines	Antidiabetic agents
Haloperidol	Cimetidine
Lithium	Methyldopa
	Inderal
	Reserpine
	Symmetrel
	Drugs with anticholinergic actions
	Others too numerous to mention

Source: Dr. Thomas D. Sabin, Boston City Hospital.

mental confusion. This man's physician consulted me after I gave a lecture in the Washington, D.C., area. I asked the doctor specifically about any drugs or medicine that John was taking, and the doctor assured me that he was perfectly healthy and took no medications whatsoever. Then he happened to think of John's allergies, and he called John's wife.

He discovered that John was on substantial doses of an antihistamine, but he tried to assure me that it was just the usual dose that he'd always been taking. However, when the doctor later reduced the amount of antihistamine, John's periods of confusion disappeared and his mental abilities returned to normal.

I think we ought to have separate dosage schedules for the elderly, just as we have for infants, because they cannot tolerate the same dosage of medication that they could at an earlier age. Only a few drug companies make allowances for the lower tolerance levels that people develop as they age, a large oversight that needs to be corrected.

I've seen the same phenomenon in a more temporary way in elderly people taking antiseasickness medication and medications that contain scopolamine. That drug used to be used in obstetrical cases to produce "twilight sleep" and painless delivery, but it really didn't produce painless delivery. What it did do was generate a loss of memory of the blessed event.

A common cause of reversible dementia in the residents Tom Sabin and I saw in Boston area nursing homes, second only to depression, was brain poisoning with various medicines that had been used to treat both psychiatric and medical problems. In any patient who has undergone a mental change, a change in personality, or impairment of memory, it's vitally important to check his or her medications and specifically to get a blood level to see if the patient is ingesting too much medicine. If the doctor declines to do this, a second medical opinion should be obtained, either from a neurologist or a psychopharmacologist. I can't emphasize enough that the amount of medicine used to treat a heart or blood pressure problem in a fifty-year-old may be too much for a person over sixty and may result in mental changes that resemble Alzheimer's disease.

My comments about brain poisons should not be misinterpreted to mean that I'm against broad classes of drugs. If a person is getting too much medication, the amount has to be reduced. If one medication, like digitalis or Inderal, causes intellectual deterioration, it has to be discontinued and another, nontoxic agent must be substituted as soon as possible. I'm not suggesting that essential heart or blood pressure medications be abandoned if they are medically indicated, but that the agent that is poisoning the brain be discontinued and a more effective, less toxic substitute be given. Sometimes when there is no alternative, a doctor will simply have to prescribe what he or she feels causes the least harmful side effects.

POISONS AROUND US

We live in an inherently dangerous world. Our air, water, and even our food may contain contaminants that cause irreparable damage to our brains. Through no fault of our own, we sometimes expose ourselves to things that will eventually kill us.

The list of pollutants and chemicals that we need to avoid is too long to list here, but I do want to discuss some of the most common toxins that you can avoid. Lead, for example, which is found in old paints (and is particularly dangerous in old buildings where the paint is flaking), is frequently ingested by children and may cause such severe brain swelling that an operation is necessary to reduce the increased pressure inside the head.

Mercury, another potent brain poison, volatilizes at room temperature and condenses on skin and the lining of the respiratory tract. In years past, the symptoms of mercury poisoning of the brain were so common in workers who made felt hats (in which mercury is used) that a phrase was coined to describe the psychological upsets they suffered: "Mad as a hatter."

Mercury is sometimes used today in tiny amounts in the amalgams for dental fillings. At present, an unresolved controversy continues about its long-term potential for producing emotional disturbances.

Arsenic and other heavy metals can also produce symptoms of brain and peripheral nerve dysfunction. These metals and a number of organic solvents, often found in industrial waste and insecticides, can contaminate water supplies or get into the food chain by being ingested by edible fish. Typically, the symptoms of poisoning include severe tremors, impaired intellectual function, hearing loss, reduced vision, and, if the poisoning is extreme enough, seizures and even coma.

Keep in mind that the presence of these types of poisons in the body is detectable if the appropriate tests are carried out and that brain poisoning as a cause of dementia is treatable. That's why it's so important for you and your physician to recognize it as a possibility when attempting to diagnose a dementing illness that has no obvious cause and to take appropriate action quickly.

Chapter 7

Brain Injuries
and Disease
(Excluding Stroke)

When I was a child of eight or nine I had an insatiable desire to read, and I read everything: telephone books, dictionaries, encyclopedias, plays by Shakespeare, and stories by Dickens. I read so rapidly that I was always looking for new material. One night my father, who was a physician, brought home some books that he was using to prepare a lecture dealing with mental illness and epilepsy. He was called away suddenly and in his absence I began leafing through the neuropsychiatric volumes filled with vivid pictures.

My attention was riveted. Here was something that fascinated me more than a Gothic novel. I was struck by the challenge and filled with a deep sympathy for the people who suffered from maladies that were so little understood and so poorly treated. The plight of those poor men and women I saw in the pictures, and those that I subsequently saw in my early medical training, spurred me on to learn more. Even years later, when I had finished my medical training and had begun my surgical education, my attention returned again and again to the problems of people who suffered from brain disease and abnormal behavior. I realized that surgery was a more direct way to develop more precise diagnoses and effective treatments for those people, and so I became a neurosurgeon.

Ever since I made that decision, I have tried to shine what light I could on the darkest corners of neurological science, areas such as dementia, massive brain injuries, and crippling brain diseases that defy quick and easy treatments. As I think back over the many kinds of disorders I've treated, I recall most clearly the victims and the great courage they displayed in the face of personal suffering and tragedy. They are the ones who inspired me to keep looking for ways to help them, and it is their desire to recover that motivates me still to forge on.

BRAIN INJURIES: A COMMON CAUSE OF BRAIN DYSFUNCTION

I was supervising two senior residents in the operating rooms of Boston City Hospital one afternoon when I received a call to report to the accident floor and meet with the commissioner of police. When I arrived I was shown into one of the emergency operating theaters where a table was occupied by a uniformed figure surrounded by a team of efficient accident floor physicians and nurses. The policeman lying there was profoundly unconscious. Tubes were going into his veins, airway, and bladder, and his head was being shaved for surgery. A laceration over his left ear showed pulsating fragments of bone, dura, and brain. Alongside the man's head was half a cup of brain tissue neatly laid on a gauze square. Someone had collected and preserved it under the false assumption that I could somehow put it back.

This traffic patrolman had been shot by an escaping jewel robber with a .38-caliber revolver at almost point-blank range in downtown Boston about seventeen minutes before I saw him. A bullet had penetrated the officer's brain.

As we were wheeling him up to my operating suite, I still remember the nursing supervisor whispering in my ear: "The commissioner wants to see you." "Later," I said. "Much later."

The high-velocity bullet had pulverized much of the motor speech area in the policeman's left (dominant) hemisphere and had torn the leash of blood vessels that feeds the sensitive area of the brain known as the middle cerebral artery. I removed the bullet and the dead tissue and stopped the bleeding. It was all I could do, but at the time I remember wondering to myself if it was even worthwhile. Would this man be able to function without his motor speech area, even if he survived this grievous injury to his brain?

Three years after he was discharged, when I saw Officer Handley again in the outpatient department, he was confined to a wheelchair most of the time. He could use his partially paralyzed right leg to walk with support, but his right arm didn't function at all and he had no speech. However, he did understand almost all commands that were said to him. He smiled and was taken care of assiduously by a young woman who became his constant companion and nurse. He enjoyed his rides out into the country, and he began to use his left hand to assist himself in activities of daily living and most functions of eating. His brain function was severely diminished, but in his own way he was able to communicate and he seemed to enjoy life. He died four years later, not from anything related to his brain injury, but from a rapidly advancing cancer of the stomach.

Incidentally, I did have a talk with the police commissioner, and he proved to be very helpful in arranging for rehabilitation therapy, special nurses, and blood donors at a time when these were critically needed for the officer.

Most head injuries that interfere with brain function aren't so dramatic. I used to think that lesser head injuries weren't important and that any time an individual injured his or her head, even though the injury might cause amnesia or unconsciousness for a brief period of time, the head injury probably wasn't significant and didn't require further attention. Subsequent investigations proved to me that I was dead wrong.

Even head injuries that I would consider to be relatively minor might impair memory and intellectual function for as long as two to three weeks after the injury, although the period of unconsciousness and amnesia was brief. Furthermore, a second head injury always produces more brain dysfunction than just one alone. In other words, the effects seem to be cumulative, with longer-lasting periods of memory loss, intellectual deterioration, and the onset of a syndrome seen most frequently in punch-drunk fighters and called by the fancy term dementia pugilistica. Alcoholics often have this syndrome because they are prone to repeated head injuries.

The most disabling symptoms of all, however, are usually emotional or psychiatric, symptoms that disrupt the victim's social, professional, and family life. This disruption can go on for many weeks to months or even years. Control studies done on people who had injuries to other parts of their bodies, such as the arms, chest, or abdomen, do not reveal such disabilities. I have a feeling that the emotional symptoms are due to an injury to the base of the brain that contains the limbic, or emotional, brain structures. I must hasten to add, however, that my idea has not been confirmed.

The kind of head injury case I often see is the sort that Harley, a plumbing contractor, suffered when he fell off a scaffolding, injuring his head and developing epileptic seizures. These were adequately treated with Dilantin and he went back to plumbing, years later going into business for himself as an independent contractor.

One evening, Harley was sitting with a building owner discussing plans for remodeling the bathrooms of an apartment building when someone came up behind him and hit him repeatedly over the head with a tire iron. He was unconscious for four or five hours and woke up in a hospital. Incredibly, Harley's tests did not show any obvious brain injury, but after he got out of the hospital he found that his ability to concentrate, to make executive decisions, and, more important, to remember events was severely disturbed. His small contracting business slipped away because he could no longer calculate or do estimates accurately. The problem was that he couldn't remember figures to make the calculations, and often his calculations were inaccurate and unreliable. Soon his wife had to go to work to support the family, he lost his federally mortgaged home, he went on relief, and he began to have episodes of seizures punctuated by periods of drinking alcohol in large amounts.

I had practically given up hope that Harley would ever recover because his episodes of seizures and drinking continued to get him into trouble. His family left him, and he also became estranged from his parents.

One day Harley came to me and said that he had hit rock bottom and wanted to do something to try to help himself. I tested him and found some encouraging signs. He seemed, for the first time, to have some improvement in his recent-memory functions. Some previously disabled circuitry had apparently reestablished itself. Healing was taking place. He went to a motivational seminar to try to get back some of his self-confidence, and he won an award for achievement. Three months later, he cautiously started a business again. The return of recent memory was accelerated; his intellectual abilities improved and his usually volatile temper was kept in check. His wife came back to live with him, and about six months later he drove up to my office in the longest Cadillac that I've ever seen, full of confidence and bubbling with enthusiasm. His business had taken off, his skills had returned, and his ability to estimate jobs was as good as ever.

Harley's story brought back the point to me that head injuries can get better with time and treatment. Five years had gone by and there had been a lot of trouble in the meanwhile, but what a recovery! He is still on medication, but his family, business, and life are back together again.

Some head injuries can be more subtle. Helena, the wife of a Philadelphia lawyer and herself an attorney, began to have symptoms of mild headaches and periods of confusion. She was seen by a neurologist who said there was nothing wrong with her, and then by a psychiatrist who explained that the butterflies she was seeing on the ceilings and walls were symptoms of deep anxiety and stress. These symptoms kept getting worse until finally she was hospitalized in one of the psychiatric units in a major East Coast teaching hospital.

Helena was a very religious woman and when she found that no one seemed to be able to help her, she started to pray, sometimes aloud. "God help me!" she cried out one night. "May God help me!" The male psychiatric nurse went over to her and said, "Stop that disturbance. I'm going to tie your hands behind your back if you keep shouting like that." The nurse was good to his word, and on two evenings Helena spent a seemingly endless night of torture with her hands tied as a punishment for her persistent loud prayers and failure to obey the ward nurse.

The next day her husband called me and said, "Doctor, I've been told my wife is going to have to go into an institution and I'm kind of sad, you know, because it will be the first time that we've been separated in forty-three years of married life. I wonder if you could see her and do an examination of her on that new special x-ray machine of yours."

Against her doctor's wishes, I did exactly that and found two substantial blood clots pressing on both sides of her brain. Because the CAT scanner was new at that time, my findings weren't believed at first. It took two days for me to convince her doctors to remove the clots. Three months later, Helena was back practicing law, as good as ever, but very outraged at her physicians.

The missed diagnosis of a blood clot, called a subdural hematoma, is not infrequent. The symptoms of subdural hematoma are similar to a lot of other dementing illnesses and are easily overlooked. More than half the people who have them don't recall any significant injury that produced the clot, and in Helena's case it was only much later that she remembered hitting her head on a shingle protruding from a roof. She had a headache at the time, but she didn't recall the incident as being particularly serious.

An accumulation of subdural hematoma is more common toward the beginning of life and in old age when there may be a disproportion between the size of the brain and the size of the skull. Although neurosurgeons see quite a few people with the disorder, those people represent a very small proportion of people who get hit on the head. The great majority of head injuries are trivial and do not produce this or any other disease. However, head injuries that do produce even short periods of unconsciousness or memory loss probably result in some loss of brain cells. Repeated brain injury has to be avoided at all costs since it will magnify any loss of brain function. Victims of repeated brain injury should consider wearing protective headgear when riding in automobiles or playing sports.

BRAIN DISEASES THAT PRODUCE DEMENTING ILLNESS

As we get older, our brains become less elastic, so that anything, even a tiny bleed into the spinal fluid, that causes an increase in pressure inside the fluid-filled spaces of the brain (the ventricles) may cause them to enlarge. When they enlarge, the pressure inside the head goes back to normal because the elastic force of the brain is diminished and the space for the brain substance decreases in size. This enlargement of the brain ventricles is called hydrocephalus ("water head"). Since the pressure remains normal in this instance, it is called normal-pressure hydrocephalus. This problem may occur in the elderly and is often treated by insertion of a shunt that diverts the spinal fluid either into the heart or into the peritoneal cavity (the abdomen) through a one-way valve.

The most frequent symptoms of this disorder are memory loss followed by incontinence and, most important, gait disturbance. The disorder can be confirmed with a CAT scan of the brain or a magnetic resonance scan, followed by a special radioactive examination of spinal fluid flow. Then surgery can be done to correct the problem. Sometimes only part of the syndrome — the abnormal gait — is improved by the surgical treatment, and the memory loss and other disabling symptoms of dementia persist. This is not because the operation doesn't successfully reduce the size of the ventricles, but because many of the people also have Alzheimer's disease. Thus the hydrocephalus can be treated but the dementing process, secondary to Alzheimer's disease, is not improved by the operation.

Most people who have normal-pressure hydrocephalus become sleepy, and a few become aggressive. One patient with the latter symptom was Herman, a fifty-eight-year-old chunky, cigar-smoking wholesale grocer. For about three years he had a progressive deterioration in his ability to walk, and his memory, which was an important asset in conducting his business, began to fail. Herman had had tests done by other neurosurgeons who thought that his enlarged ventricles were related to some birth injury and that he had a primary psychiatric disease that caused him to become aggressive, especially toward his wife. He also had partial complex seizures, which were treated with Tegretol, an anticonvulsant. The medication did not help his symptoms, however.

Shunting his spinal fluid into his peritoneal cavity did help. At first his peritoneal cavity didn't seem to absorb the spinal fluid and his belly began to protrude ominously. Finally his body readjusted to the new demands of this fluid transfer and he was able to function efficiently in his business, had no headaches, and began walking normally again. Most important, his abnormal aggression also stopped.

BRAIN TUMORS

We tend to think that brain tumors are more common than they really are because they are often given a lot of media attention. I find that only one or two people out of a hundred who come to see me because of memory or intellectual loss actually have a brain tumor. However, when tumors do occur, they are serious matters. People who have brain tumors may experience dementing symptoms if their frontal lobe is invaded or destroyed by the tumor; but they usually also have such symptoms as paralysis, seizures, loss of vision or hearing, headaches, and increased pressure inside the head because of the mass growing in the confined volume of the cranial cavity. Occasionally, when the tumor irritates the emotional brain, behavioral symptoms will also occur.

This was the case with Rudy, a forty-two-year-old car salesman who had had occasional headaches and transient weakness in one arm and leg. When he was seen by the neurology service at a major teaching hospital he was told there was nothing physically wrong with him, and he was sent to see a psychiatrist. The psychiatrist, interestingly, thought Rudy might have a brain tumor, but he took no action to confirm that hunch. Rudy did not return to the hospital until nine o'clock one night when he was brought in by police officers and fire fighters in a net, kicking, shouting, and biting like a wild animal. Rudy had suddenly gone berserk, wielding a meat cleaver over his head and threatening to decapitate his wife and daughter, who went screaming onto the streets of East Boston.

After Rudy was given an injection to calm him, I was able to look at his optic nerve heads with an ophthalmoscope, and I saw that they were swollen as a result of increased pressure inside the brain. I didn't have a CAT scan to rely on then, so I injected a radiopaque dye into the artery going into his brain and took special x-rays that showed that he had a brain tumor about the size of a half grapefruit pressing on the bottom of his frontal lobe and the tip of his temporal lobe. It was a benign tumor called a meningioma, but it had a very rich blood supply and I succeeded in getting it all out, with some difficulty.

I followed Rudy's case for about thirty-five years, and he never had another violent attack. The deterioration in brain function that he'd had before, with wild, unmanageable behavior, was significantly reversed and improved. He stopped working as a car salesman and spent his working life as a claims adjuster with notable success until he retired.

Rudy's wife never slept in the same room with him, much to his amazement — he had no recollection of events that occurred at the time of his brain decompensation. His wife kept her door locked and was always a little anxious around him. In fact, she brought him to see me recently, saying that he was off again and had attacked her. Apparently, they were walking home from the movie theater and he tripped on some uneven sidewalk. He reached over to try to steady himself, but when she saw his hand coming she began to scream and ran away in fright. I assured her that Rudy would do her no harm, but I don't think she believed me.

I'm often surprised at how long it can take for some people to seek medical treatment for a brain tumor, even when they have very noticeable symptoms. A male nurse, who most certainly should have known to seek help early, consulted me after he experienced difficulty walking. He also discovered that he couldn't read a postcard and was said by his roommate to be sleeping all the time. In fact, he had become profoundly demented. Special x-rays showed the reason for this gradual but severe decline in his memory, executive functions, and ability to sustain intellectual effort. He had a huge olfactory groove meningioma, a benign tumor that compressed and displaced almost all of one frontal lobe and more than a third of the other frontal lobe after the tumor had crossed the midline of the brain.

The operation revealed that his frontal lobes were substantially destroyed by the tumor, and yet after this mass was removed he recovered a substantial amount of function and was able to go back into nursing. He continued to have interpersonal problems in his relationships with other nurses, however, because he was short-tempered and somewhat insensitive to his fellow workers. But he was pleasant to his patients, especially young children and the elderly.

BRAIN INFECTIONS

Like tumors, an infection of the brain can cause a loss of intellectual function whether the infection is generalized or whether it takes the form of an abscess, which may actually mimic symptoms and signs of a brain tumor. The best-known infectious disease that changes personality and reduces intellectual ability is syphilis of the brain. Part of the madness of gangster Al Capone was caused by this disease. Most often, syphilis causes a deterioration and shrinkage of the frontal lobes, but occasionally it forms a hard, rubbery tumor called a gumma. Structurally, a gumma from a syphilitic infection is very similar to a tuberculoma (a tumor produced by tuberculosis).

I once operated on a woman who was five months pregnant, and who had signs of increasing intercranial pressure and intellectual deterioration. She had a large tumor that was in one frontal lobe and extended back into the motor speech area. The tumor was about three centimeters underneath the surface of her brain and when I probed it, I could feel its tough, resilient character.

Before cutting into the brain to remove the tumor, I noticed that there was a peculiar white, mottled discoloration along the blood vessels on the surface of the brain. I carefully removed one of these tiny areas and sent it to the brain pathologist for a frozen section. His diagnosis came back: tuberculosis. On that basis, I decided not to try to remove the tumor, which was in all likelihood a tuberculoma, but decided instead to decompress the patient and treat her with antituberculosis drugs.

I left her bone flap out (storing it under sterile conditions at low temperature in a blood bank) and fashioned a large pocket of fascia around the opening of the dura matter to relieve the increased intercranial pressure in the brain. After six weeks of antituberculosis therapy, her brain no longer bulged. She subsequently delivered a normal child, and all signs of her tuberculoma had resolved about four and a half months after delivery. Fortunately, there was no need to remove a tumor and all I had to do was to replace the bone flap.

The virus that causes AIDS also produces a degenerative disease of the brain associated with memory loss and apathy. The first physicians who treated AIDS patients incorrectly thought that this brain infection was really a sign of severe depression. It's difficult at times to differentiate between the apathy of frontal lobe deterioration and psychomotor retardation caused by depression. But it was obvious that there were other kinds of intellectual changes present in AIDS patients that were associated with rapid shrinkage of the brain. We have since learned that the loss of intellectual abilities in some infected persons may precede any overt sign of immune disease, and, more important, the loss of brain function, at least temporarily, is reversible with proper medication.

A twenty-seven-year-old woman with PCP pneumonia, a complication of AIDS, was thought to be profoundly demented, and her physicians at Boston City Hospital did not know whether it was worthwhile to treat her with the new drug AZT. The woman was able to speak only a few words in a non-English dialect, and she seemed to have poor intellectual ability. After three weeks of AZT therapy, however, her PCP pneumonia resolved, but, more important, she showed a striking change in her mental abilities. She was able to speak quite well in three languages (two of which we mistakenly thought she didn't know). This kind of result speaks for making an early diagnosis of HIV infection. If brain infection does occur, it can be reversed with medication rather than being allowed to advance to its end stages, when it produces a dramatic shrinkage in the brain as seen on CAT scan.

At times, an infection with a fungus, such as cryptococcus, can cause an inflammatory reaction in the meninges, the membranes surrounding the brain, with some backup of spinal fluid and expansion of the ventricles. This happened to a South Carolina veterinarian who went repeatedly to a neurological clinic to try to find out why he was losing his intellectual abilities. The doctors did everything — CAT scan, MRI, blood studies, repeated neurological examination, psychological tests — and they couldn't come up with a definite diagnosis.

The man found that he was getting progressively worse and he demanded to be seen again. Finally, his doctors did a spinal puncture and they saw the offending organism, the cryptococcus, in an examination of the spinal fluid. Medical treatment finally produced a substantial improvement.

Almost any infectious agent, bacteria, spirochete, fungus, or virus can infect the brain and produce symptoms of loss of function. Even the herpes virus can occasionally infect the temporal lobes, leading to a dementing and life-threatening inflammation of the brain.

PARKINSON'S DISEASE

There are a number of primary diseases of the brain, such as Huntington's chorea (an inherited familial movement disorder with frontal lobe and basal ganglia dysfunction), Pick's disease (an Alzheimer-like syndrome affecting the temporal and frontal lobes), and even multiple sclerosis, which can cause damage to the white matter of the frontal lobe and diminish intellectual function.

But it is Parkinson's disease, a disorder associated with loss of the neurotransmitter dopamine in the basal ganglia of the brain, that is most likely to send a patient into a nursing home. In its late stages, Parkinson's produces a substantial loss of intellectual function, and it is associated with rigidity of movement, a tremor of the hands at rest, and a peculiar inability to initiate movement. Unlike the results in Alzheimer's disease, the CAT scan in Parkinson's disease has a good correlation with the degree of intellectual loss or dementia — that is, the greater the loss of brain tissue, particularly of the inner parts of the brain, the more likely the person is to have a substantial loss of intellectual function. (In Alzheimer's disease, the loss of intellectual function is likely to be correlated only with expansion of the fluid-filled space in the center of the brain on a CAT scan.)

It is curious that many Alzheimer patients, late in the course of their disease, develop symptoms like those of Parkinson's disease. One differentiating feature between advanced Alzheimer's disease with the Parkinson's syndrome and end-stage Parkinson's disease with dementia is that in the latter condition, disability with language function, such as naming objects, is unusual, whereas it is common in Alzheimer's disease. And in Parkinson patients, the movement disorder is seen first and intellectual deterioration occurs in later stages of the disease. If one sees these two syndromes late in the course of the illness, without having prior knowledge of how they began, they often look quite similar.

Years ago, before the introduction of more effective anti-Parkinson medications, I and many other neurosurgeons used to operate on people with Parkinson's disease and make destructive lesions in the inner parts of their brains to relieve the rigidity of their limbs and the abnormal tremors. Our surgery didn't do much for their inability to initiate movement, called akinesia, but a drug called L-dopa, given in rather massive amounts by physician George Cotzias, who nearly two decades ago was working under the supervision of my old chief William Sweet at the Brookhaven National Hospital, was able to correct the akinesia very dramatically. Indeed, Cotzias's contribution revolutionized the treatment of Parkinson's disease.

At first, people were talking about a cure, but that was much too optimistic. What Cotzias was able to do with the drug in the early stages of the disease was to replace the neurotransmitter dopamine that was lacking in certain target areas inside the Parkinson patient's brain. Unfortunately, the disease is progressive, with loss of nerve tissue, and after some years the L-dopa is no longer effective.

Some researchers thought that the drug's eventual ineffectiveness was caused by the brain's inability to transform L-dopa into the end product dopamine. (L-dopa has to be given instead of dopamine itself because when dopamine is given intravenously it causes an unacceptable rise in blood pressure and it doesn't penetrate the blood-brain barrier to produce therapeutic levels in the target areas of the brain.) In 1982 the thinking was that the L-dopa was being transformed into something besides the dopamine that was toxic to the brain. I and a team of neurosurgeons and neurologists under Tom Sabin thought we could get around this problem by putting a tiny catheter inside the spaces of the brain, the ventricles, allowing dopamine to drip directly on the end organs that form the undersurface of the anterior ventricles in the brain. A man with hopelessly advanced Parkinson's disease volunteered as a subject for this medical experiment, and the whole process was approved by an institutional review board and ethics committee.

Temporarily at least, the man's symptoms of Parkinson's disease were improved, but when we tried to give him a higher dosage of dopamine he became psychotic, with hallucinations, and we had to abandon the therapy. We learned from doing the procedure that dopamine itself, not some intermediate compound, could evoke delusions and hallucinations.

Some neurosurgeons in Sweden are now using a controversial method known as fetal transplants of adrenal medulla to replace the dopamine in the target areas deep in the brain, and neurosurgeons in Mexico are using fetal nerve cell transplants to attempt the same procedure. I think we are all stymied at this point because the important cells that must receive the dopamine have degenerated. I believe that if we're going to make any headway we must have some way of replacing those cells. Maybe the fetal nerve cell procedure will be the answer. We certainly need a new technique because when brain cells deteriorate we have no way to replace them. Fetal nerve cell transplants give us at least the theoretical possibility of achieving what was previously thought to be impossible.

TREATMENTS FOR OTHER DEGENERATIVE BRAIN DISEASES

Some rare or uncommon genetic or familial degenerative brain diseases that produce dementia are today becoming treatable or reversible. One example is Wilson's disease, which is associated with degeneration of the inner parts of the brain and portions of the liver. The symptoms of this disease begin during the second decade of life, starting with a tremor of a limb and sometimes of the head, slowness of movement, difficulty formulating words and swallowing, hoarseness, and occasional unusual postures of the limbs. At times, the victim may exhibit an abnormality of behavior such as being excessively emotional or argumentative, and a loss of intellectual function may occur.

As Wilson's disease progresses, increased difficulty swallowing, with drooling as well as rigidity, slowness in initiating movements, and resting tremors, which are very coarse and are called wing-beating tremors, occur. There is often an unusual rusty-brown discoloration in the deepest layer of the cornea. Basic research discovered that symptoms come about from an inherited defect that produces an unusual accumulation of copper in the tissues. Investigators have now found drugs to prevent the absorption of copper and thus help reduce symptoms. Dietary reduction of copper, to less than 1 mg per day, through the avoidance of cocoa, nuts, shellfish, mushrooms, and liver, and the administration of an agent that binds the copper, called D-penicillamine, often produces a steady and marked improvement. Liver function returns to normal, abnormal brain signs improve dramatically, and the unusual discoloration in the eye, called a Kayser-Fleisher ring, disappears.

The more we understand about the cause and mechanism of various disease states, whether they be infectious, metabolic, vascular, inherited, or sporadic, the greater chance we have of devising effective treatments. This is especially true for demyelinating diseases associated with a loss of myelin sheath from some nerve fibers in the brain. Although some demyelinating diseases such as multiple sclerosis usually do not produce a loss of intellectual function in the early stages, repeated episodes of demyelination may produce a steady advance of this disorder that eventually may disrupt frontal lobe connections and functions and produce apathy and loss of intellectual abilities. Other kinds of demyelinating disease (resulting in a more extensive loss of the myelin sheath around axons or nerve fibers in the brain) are more explosive and produce a rapid loss of brain function. Fortunately, the more rapidly developing disorders are uncommon.

My good friend the late psychiatrist Leo Alexander started the use of steroids to retard the course of multiple sclerosis. At first people laughed at him and said that he was just using a psychiatric or emotional placebo effect to help his patients. But he persisted, and now many people realize that the judicious use of steroids can be very helpful in prolonging the periods of symptom-free existence and in diminishing the recurrent attacks of numbness, double vision, weakness, or bladder dysfunction that characterize the disease. We are learning more and more about multiple sclerosis every day, and I have no doubt that in the next five or ten years we're going to come up with more effective treatments.

EPILEPSY

One of the ways to think about the brain is as an electrochemical machine. Several kinds of electrical signals can be recorded from electrodes in the brain, on the brain, or, more commonly, on the scalp. One signal response is time-locked to the stimulus and varies depending on whether the specific environmental stimulus is a flash of light or the sound of clicking in the ear. In other words, a signal response follows each stimulus in an identical time-locked relationship. Another kind of electrical signal that can be recorded from the brain is not directly related to environmental stimuli but consists of an alteration in the potential or voltage within the brain as a function of time. If this alteration is recorded on an oscilloscope screen or an ink-writer, it appears as a wavy line that oscillates up and down in a wave pattern as time passes. (Time is measured in very small increments: milliseconds for the time-locked signals and fractions of a second for the oscillating potentials.)

The oscillations of the brain wave form a pattern, or signature, which is easily recognized, with frequencies and voltages that fall into a normal range of values. When the brain wave amplitude (or height of the wave on the screen) increases sharply, producing either a spike or a sharp wave, or when the frequency (the number of times a complete wave appears within a certain distance left to right on the screen) slows down or speeds up too much, it indicates that the electrochemical machine — the brain — is not working properly. When an electrical recording from someone's brain is associated with a lapse of consciousness, it may form a pattern of very slow or very rapid high-amplitude spikes that can be the sign of a seizure or convulsion.

When most people think of an epileptic seizure, they picture someone falling down on the ground, frothing at the mouth, jerking the arms and legs, and turning blue. After the seizure, the victim is often confused and suffers some memory loss. That is the classic picture of a major seizure, or grand mal convulsion. There are also minor seizures with just small lapses in consciousness; these are seen particularly in children. In adults, minor seizures may produce twitching only in an isolated limb or part of the face, or they may produce an abnormal sensation in a part of the body, an abnormal vision, or even the aura of an unusual smell, taste, or sound. Since minor seizures often don't develop into grand mal seizures, they are called partial seizures. And because they may consist of a variety of symptoms — visual, motor, sensory — they are called complex.

Complex partial seizures occur most frequently in the temporal brain, just deep to the ear, especially in the deep part of that brain which is part of the limbic or emotional system. When they originate there they may generate changes in behavior or feelings as part of the seizure pattern. Karen, the twenty-two-year-old daughter of a physics professor at a midwestern university, had exactly this problem. She was brought to see me because her partial complex seizures sometimes ended in aggressive or violent behavior — random muscular activity that ended in violence more by accident than by intent.

Before I go into more detail about Karen's eventual diagnosis and treatment, I want to warn you not to jump to conclusions that all epileptics, particularly people with complex partial seizures, exhibit aggressive or violent behavior. Only those people who have abnormalities of the limbic brain have behavioral or emotional changes. Karen had widespread brain disease, but the most symptom-producing lesions were in her emotional or limbic brain.

When Karen was eighteen months old, she had an inflammation of the brain as a result of a bout of the measles. This left her severely brain-damaged, with repeated grand mal convulsions, a loss of intellectual function, and strange or asocial tendencies.

At the age of eight or nine she began to have partial seizures, which started with an aura of a bad smell and continued with staring, grimacing, and attack behavior. Sometimes she became very fearful during these attacks and began to run, ending up in strange and dangerous sections of the city. Karen was often in the habit of reaching for a small dinner knife as soon as warning of a seizure came upon her so that she could defend herself if she came to her senses in an unfamiliar part of town.

When she was thirteen or fourteen she began to have increasing episodes of violence in which she smashed up her room and tried to kill herself by cutting her wrists. She also had hallucinations in which she heard voices and saw threatening figures. Her small staring spells became more frequent and after each one she became confused and had a loss of memory that made it difficult for her to orient herself to the ongoing activities of daily living. Because she was so dangerous at home, her family had her institutionalized from time to time, and during one of these spells she stabbed a nurse in the lung with a pair of scissors.

Karen was given a variety of anti-epilepsy medications and a series of major and minor tranquilizers, antidepressants, and psychotherapy, all to no avail. Because of her frequent staring spells, she was unable to accomplish any meaningful intellectual activity and was considered mentally retarded.

The fact that her problem stemmed from her limbic brain was proved after I inserted electrodes into the limbic portion of her temporal lobe and recorded and stimulated through the use of remote telemetering devices, the same technology that NASA uses in communicating with the astronauts in space. Out of thirty-six points stimulated in her limbic brain, only one initiated her seizures with the facial grimacing and ended with the undirected attack behavior. After the first stimulation, Karen hit her fist violently against the wall, and when the stimulus was applied the second time as she was playing the guitar, she swung it recklessly, narrowly missing the head of an examining psychiatrist.

The areas of her brain that provoked the abnormal responses

were inactivated by a precise heat lesion that was produced by passing a small amount of radiofrequency current through the appropriate parts of the brain electrode. In the first two or three months after the lesion, Karen rapidly gained weight from overeating and temporarily lost her musical abilities. Over the next three to four months, she made steady improvement. Her weight came back down to normal, she stopped her aggressive attacks, and the frequency of her seizures was diminished. She still required antiseizure medication and medications to control her hallucinations. It's not surprising that this was the case, since her entire brain had been afflicted by the disease process when she was eighteen months old. It was certainly unlikely that a single tiny lesion of the brain would cure or eliminate all of her symptoms, but the reduction in the number of her seizures allowed her to be less confused and to have much less memory loss. She was able to go back to studying and earned her equivalency diploma from high school. She began to compose songs and play the harp, and she volunteered to begin working for the local epilepsy society. When her father suffered a heart attack, she was able to stay at home and nurse him through the worst part of his disability.

Over thirty-eight years, I have seen more than a thousand epileptic people and have performed the kind of surgery I did on Karen only about twenty times. Most epileptic patients can be controlled with various medications: Dilantin, Tegretol, and valproate are some that I frequently use. Furthermore, even when people have epilepsy beginning in the limbic brain, it is more usual for them to have behavioral symptoms between seizures rather than during the actual spells.

The late Professor Norman Geschwind of Harvard University made a study of limbic epilepsy victims and found that they had a whole constellation of personality changes secondary to the disorder in their emotional brain. These personality features consisted of such things as hyperreligiosity, hyposexuality, compulsive writing or talking about their illness, and a reduced threshold for aggressive behavior.

Unlike people who have a defect in the anterior portion of their frontal lobe and who anger and forget their anger very quickly, people with limbic epilepsy hold a grudge and often when they feel they've been slighted, they ruminate about the supposed insult until they become more and more angry and finally explode with unrestrained emotional behavior.

Not all people with the constellation of these symptoms have obvious epilepsy or convulsions. Tommy was eighteen years old when he rode his motorcycle in the Maine countryside, encountered a deep gully in the road, and fell over his handlebars, breaking his nose. He was taken to the local hospital, where the physicians felt he had other facial fractures that required the care of a specialist, so they sent him in an ambulance to a major medical center. En route, the ambulance was involved in a head-on collision with a bus and Tommy was rendered profoundly unconscious with a severe brain injury. For several days doctors thought that Tommy wouldn't survive, but when he did recover this mild-mannered boy turned into a raging maniac with delusions, hallucinations, and overt aggressive behavior.

Tommy was heavily sedated for weeks, and when his parents took him home they couldn't sleep safely at night because, when he was able to, he got out of his bed and tried to attack them. He finally spent years in seclusion in a state mental hospital where medications, psychotherapy, and even electroshock treatment were unsuccessfully tried.

Tommy was referred to me by his neurosurgeon, who didn't know what to do with him. He was the first person without symptoms of epilepsy into whom I inserted electrodes in the limbic brain for the diagnosis and possible treatment of aggressive behavior. X-ray studies of his brain showed substantial loss of tissue in both the frontal and temporal regions, and psychological and neuropsychological tests showed that he had a far-reaching loss of intellectual and memory abilities. When he was seen by my colleague Norm Geschwind, Tommy had never had an epileptic seizure. Yet Geschwind predicted that we would find a discharging electrical focus in his limbic brain, and he was right.

Electrodes confirmed one spot in Tommy's brain that was discharging abnormally, and when we destroyed that area with a heat lesion, his violent behavior stopped and his memory improved.

Unfortunately, Tommy was so severely disabled that, just as with Karen, I was not able to reverse his medical problem simply by making a small lesion in his brain. But the lesion did make a difference. He was able to work in a sheltered workshop, he graduated from high school, and he got a license to drive a car. In fact, on one of his office visits he drove his parents down to see me from their home in Maine.

Epileptic seizures can occur at any age, not only as a result of brain poisoning with alcohol or cocaine, brain injury, brain tumors, or brain abscesses, but also as a consequence of stroke in the elderly. Anyone who is subject to seizures, even the small staring spells that are easily overlooked, may have episodes of confusion and memory loss that are directly related to the seizures. When these seizures are treated — and they usually can be effectively treated by a medical regimen using antiseizure medication — the periods of confusion decrease and the memory loss substantially improves, even in advanced old age.

Chapter 8

Medical Problems
That Alter Brain Function

The brain, spinal cord, and peripheral nerves are the most important organs in the body because they are the organs of behavior, emotion, thinking, and feeling. They are the mechanism that allows us to communicate with the outside world and that tells us what is happening inside our own bodies. They embody the unique characteristics that give us our individual identity and signature.

The brain does not work alone, however; it is supported by the other organ systems in the body. If, for example, the heart isn't pumping efficiently, or if the blood vessels don't carry the blood to and from the brain, or if the blood doesn't contain enough red blood cells or hemoglobin to bind oxygen, or if the lungs don't work efficiently in providing oxygen to be transported to the brain, then brain function is going to be altered. Furthermore, electrolytes, minerals, nutrients, and metabolites have to be kept at optimal levels to ensure adequate brain function. In short, the brain is not an island unto itself.

We see the interdependencies more clearly when we notice that even changes in an organ such as the liver can produce an unhealthy rise in ammonia circulating in the bloodstream, which can cause profound depression and alterations of brain function and a peculiar tremor. Similarly, the hormones secreted by the various endocrine glands, including the pituitary, the adrenals, the thyroid and parathyroids, and the pancreas, all play a role in regulating brain function, and disturbances in these organs and in the level of hormones they secrete can change behavior and produce intellectual loss.

The most frequent alterations in brain function as a result of hormone imbalance are produced by variations in the insulin secretion of the islands of Langerhans in the pancreas. An inadequate supply of insulin can cause diabetes mellitus, which can produce a diabetic coma. Too much insulin profoundly depresses blood sugar levels and can result in major abnormalities in brain function and even convulsions. Some people under stress get an outpouring of insulin and abnormally low blood sugar, with tremulousness, a sinking feeling, pallor and sweating, and even nausea. This condition is called reactive hypoglycemia, and it sometimes occurs in students who are agitated when taking a test. Students with the condition won't do well, but the problem can be corrected through diet.

Just how important the body's regulatory organs are to brain power was impressed upon me when I saw Jeremy, a fifty-seven-year-old unemployed shipping clerk. I first met him at the Northview Nursing Home; his bathrobe was dirty, and he looked dull, listless, and drowsy. Jeremy's speech seemed to be slurred and was almost unintelligible, and at times he became very irritable and paranoid. He slept a good deal of the time and complained of not being able to remember things; indeed, the nursing home attendants had to give him increasing care because he forgot to do the most simple things in his daily routine.

Jeremy had been in the nursing home for about three months, during which time his abilities declined rapidly. He had been transferred there from a rooming house when a friend said he couldn't take care of himself and he didn't pick up his social security check to pay his rent. The nursing home physician, Dr. DeStefano, ran a series of tests on Jeremy to see if he could discover why he was losing his intellectual faculties. One test came back positive for hypothyroidism (abnormally low thyroid function), a fairly frequent cause of intellectual loss. Replacement treatment with thyroid hormone produced a substantial improvement.

Physicians usually recognize persons with the opposite syndrome, *hyper*thyroidism, because they are likely to be irritable, apprehensive, and often quite agitated. Some may become manic and overtalkative with a flight of ideas and then have sharp mood swings with depression and weeping. They often get hallucinations. These psychotic symptoms may not be immediately resolved by treating the hyperthyroidism but usually disappear after a few months. Hypothyroidism, by contrast, and the mental changes it produces of dementia and depression are more difficult to identify. It wasn't unusual, therefore, that Jeremy's problem was not immediately spotted. But among endocrine disorders (disorders of glands such as the thyroid and pituitary), it is fairly common.

Another example of an endocrine disorder that is difficult to diagnose was related to me by a colleague, an internist who was called in to see his own aunt when she developed recurrent psychiatric symptoms that didn't respond to antidepressant medication. Her psychiatrist was frankly puzzled, and the doctors that he had brought to see the woman in consultation were not helpful. They couldn't understand why her seeming prolonged depression and agitated behavior with confusion and irritability were different from the previous attacks that she had had, which seemed to respond quickly to medication. My colleague found that his aunt had a low blood pressure and that her skin was more darkly pigmented than it had been before. Simple blood tests showed a markedly depressed sodium level.

Much to the embarrassment of the woman's attending physicians, she was found to have Addison's disease, a hypofunction of the surface layers of the adrenal gland. This is a reversible syndrome that President John F. Kennedy had. It is treatable with steroids, and it is considered a less common cause of mental change than thyroid disease. My colleague gave a word of caution to his aunt's physicians, however, to be careful with her replacement therapy of steroids. Sometimes the steroids themselves can produce a mental disturbance during the period of treatment. Since his aunt had already had a series of depressive episodes, he wanted to be certain that the therapy was handled more effectively than the diagnosis.

Depressed kidney function can result in a retention of waste products, such as urea, in the blood, which in turn exacerbates mental disturbances and memory loss. I have seen patients in kidney failure who became stuporous. The elevation of potassium in the blood sometimes caused their hearts to stop. When kidney failure or a urinary tract obstruction from an enlarged prostate occurs in someone who is already slightly demented from stroke or early stages of Alzheimer's, the loss of intellectual abilities may be profound and sudden. This may be the only sign that some new medical problem has occurred. Prompt treatment may reverse some of the lost brain function; late diagnosis and treatment are often ineffective in restoring mental capacity.

STROKE AND HEART DISEASE

Strokes, one of the most common causes of dementia, are usually included under the general heading of brain disease rather than medical problems, but in fact they are caused by a disease of the blood vessels going to and within the brain rather than of the brain tissue itself. The vital avenues of blood transmission, the arteries, have to be clear and free of obstruction so that a sufficient amount of blood circulates through the capillary bed of the brain. The same disease that produces a heart attack — an occlusion or narrowing of the blood vessels of the heart — may also produce narrowing or occlusion of the blood vessels of the brain. It's not uncommon to find that someone has one of these conditions followed by the other.

Heart attacks, if they kill a significant amount of muscle tissue in the heart wall, may also set up the physical conditions for blood clots to be present in the inner lining of the heart. Little pieces of these clots can break off and produce emboli (small particles) that go into the blood circulation of the brain and occlude the flow of blood. The same thing can occur when there is a buildup of atherosclerotic plaques in the great blood vessels of the neck, the carotid and vertebral arteries, going to the brain. As in the heart, the little pieces of clot can break off from the plaques and form emboli that travel to the brain. In some patients this process can happen repeatedly, as it did in the case of Ted, whom I saw in a small community hospital.

Ted was fifty-two years old and looked at least twenty years older. He had a shuffling gait and one could hear his slippered feet dragging along the hallway long before he himself appeared. He had had a progressive loss of memory and intellectual abilities for about six years, but he hadn't experienced the continuous decline in function that Alzheimer patients experience. He seemed to be all right one day and then he would wake up the next morning confused, irritable, and somewhat disoriented. He'd improve a bit for a week or a month, or even two or three months, and then have another episode.

What was happening was that tiny clots were breaking off from the plaques in the great vessels of his neck and were floating up to his brain until they came to a blood vessel that was too small for them to pass through. Then they would occlude that blood vessel, causing death of a tiny amount of brain tissue irrigated in that part of the blood circulation. Such a loss of brain tissue caused by deprivation of blood is called an infarct. Strangely, Ted had never had a major stroke or infarct in which he became paralyzed or speechless, and he'd never had a brain hemorrhage in which a blood vessel actually burst. The part of the brain that was lost was usually the deeper part, and the space that was created by the death of brain tissue was filled by the expansion of the ventricles, the fluid-filled spaces inside the brain. The symptoms produced by these little strokes would consist of transient episodes of confusion, memory loss, and personality change, and after each episode his level of recovery would leave him with decreasing intellectual abilities.

When we took his first CAT scans we actually didn't see any of these little infarcts. His scan showed only an enlargement of the ventricles. But when we examined the x-rays very carefully we found one little area next to his ventricles in which there was a loss of tissue. Another embolus had produced a very small infarct, and it was readily observable.

The disease that Ted was suffering from is called multi-infarct dementia, in which a number of tiny strokes occur either because small blood vessels close off or because emboli float into the blood circulation and close off blood vessels. This is a very frequent cause of dementia; it afflicts thousands of people and is, at least theoretically, preventable. Sometimes the source of emboli in the great blood vessels of the neck can be eliminated by surgery; at other times, anticlotting medicine can be used to stop the clots from embolizing the blood vessels in the brain. Often, this disease is confused with Alzheimer's syndrome and nothing is done to try to correct it or to stop more spare emboli from entering the brain circulation. After repeated embolic infarcts, brain destruction becomes extensive and loss of brain function is irreversible. Since the condition is treatable if diagnosed early, all physicians who treat patients over the age of fifty should be more aware of it.

Larger strokes involving substantial areas of the cortex (the surface layers of the brain) can produce paralysis or loss of speech. If they are extensive enough, they may also generate a loss of intellectual function, as was the case with Marcel, a seventy-eight-year-old man who was placed in a nursing home with great reluctance by his religious wife when his behavior became unbearable. About five years before, he had had a major stroke that had destroyed much of one temporal lobe. He had lost a significant amount of speech but had recovered some function, including the ability to walk, with a steady and determined effort.

After three years, he went into a teaching hospital to have a prostate operation, which was accomplished without incident. But after surgery Marcel was noted to be confused and disoriented. He stopped using eating utensils and began eating with his hands. He also put almost any objects within his reach, including napkins, spoons, or flowers, into his mouth and began chewing on them. Although he had great difficulty getting about and was mostly confined to a wheelchair, he made lunging and clumsy sexual advances to most of the women who came to give him nursing care. This change in character disgusted his wife; it was the one kind of behavior that she wouldn't tolerate. That was when she placed him in a nursing home.

The nursing home doctors thought his behavior was so unusual that they brought him into the hospital for me and my partner to diagnose. We found that he had Bucy Kluver syndrome, which is related to the destruction of both anterior temporal lobes. We predicted that this would be the finding on a CAT scan, and indeed there was an infarct in the previously undamaged temporal lobe that must have happened soon after his prostate surgery. Unfortunately, there wasn't much that we could do to repair the damage to his brain caused by the infarcts, but at least his wife was somewhat mollified when she understood that the cause of his changed behavior was a stroke and not a sudden loss of faith or change in his character.

Marcel's case does point out an important lesson: that sudden changes in personality require immediate and extensive brain examinations. Furthermore, a person who has had one stroke should always be considered susceptible to having another, and any major surgical procedure, unless it is an emergency, should not be carried out without determining how to reduce the risk of a subsequent stroke.

CANCER: PHYSICAL EFFECTS ON
BRAIN POWER FUNCTION

Any major disease of the body, whether it is an infection, a heart attack, or cancer, may be accompanied by a profound change in mood and a serious depression. For cancer victims, this personality change is caused by more than the knowledge that they have a dangerous and possibly fatal disease. It is a response or reaction of the body to serious illness. Furthermore, certain kinds of cancers, such as oat cell cancers of the lung, are associated with an inflammatory and degenerative disease of the brain that is not a result of metastatic spread of cancer cells. A confusional, agitated state with hallucinations and loss of recent memory is often associated with certain cancers. The reason for this change and inflammation is not immediately clear.

A more common cause of intellectual change is produced by a metastatic brain cancer that arises from a primary cancer in, for example, the lung or breast. Brain metastases should always be considered in a person with known carcinoma who gets symptoms of memory loss or a change in personality, paralysis, or seizures. Brain metastasis is more likely to occur when the primary tumor is in the lung, breast, thyroid, or kidney than when it is in the bowel.

Frieda, a forty-seven-year-old piano teacher with a known lung cancer that had been removed, experienced a marked behavioral change as her cancer progressed. Usually lung cancer produces many metastases in the brain and so other treatments besides surgery have to be considered. In Frieda's case, she had a very early warning that something was amiss: She found that her right hand became clumsy when she was playing the piano, a particularly upsetting development to her because her hands were vital to her work and life's joy.

Special x-rays showed a small mass lesion in the part of her brain that controlled movement in her right hand. No other tumors were seen and so I elected to operate on the lesion. I exposed the cortex of her brain and found one area that was discolored, thin, and almost translucent. Then I incised the covering of the discolored area and fluid spilled out, exposing a well-encapsulated metastatic tumor that could be removed with no difficulty and no damage to the surrounding areas.

Frieda was delighted with the results of the surgery: She was able to go back to playing the piano and teaching students. Most people with metastatic cancer of the lung don't survive very long, but Frieda went more than five years before she had any new trouble.

The symptoms produced by a metastatic cancer of the brain are similar to the symptoms of a primary brain tumor except that the onset of a cancer is often more abrupt and the spread of the disease more rapid. The kind of symptoms that are produced depends on the location and size of the tumor and on whether it destroys brain tissue or irritates it and generates an epileptic seizure.

Tumors in the front part of the brain can produce sudden changes in personality, taking the form of either a loss of inhibitions and a coarsening of behavior or an apathy that can be confused with early Alzheimer's disease or depression. Clearly in such cases, the sooner a diagnosis is made, the sooner effective treatments can begin, and the better the long-term prognosis will be.

PAIN

Chronic pain has very disabling effects on the human body, usually generating a severe depression that makes the pain worse and interferes with normal brain function. Napoleon, a house painter who had a well-deserved reputation as a lecher and alcohol abuser, had always worked intermittently with great energy, drunk with great gusto, and then returned to his family abusive and irritable.

He made life very unpleasant for his wife and five children until he was discovered to have a cancer of his tongue. Numerous treatments were ineffective in stopping the growth, which spread to sensitive nerve endings in the base of his skull and gave him overwhelming and continuous pain. Napoleon became severely depressed, even to the extent that he stopped drinking. Nevertheless, he continued to be nasty and cold to his wife and children.

Medication did not help his pain, and he was referred to me for an operation on his brain. Because he had a substantial depression associated with decreased intellectual ability, I elected to put an electrode in a part of the brain that controls mood, and I made a tiny heat lesion in this area, which resulted in a dramatic change. Afterward, Napoleon's depression and pain evaporated and with it went his bad temper and abusive treatment of his family.

Everyone was amazed and pleased with the change in him when he went home. He had changed from an unrelenting tyrant into a pleasant, helpful, caring husband and father. He brought presents for his children and helped his wife around the home with cooking and household chores.

Some months later, when Napoleon came back into the hospital with a far advanced and fatally enlarged mass in his tongue, he tried to cheer up his family by cajoling them and telling them jokes. His behavior in the hospital was so magnanimous that he became a favorite of the nurses and doctors, and when he died the chief of psychiatry at the hospital was so distressed that he openly cried. I, too, was sad to see him go, although the same could not have been said of him before his personality change.

STRESS

In this chapter I have talked about the effects on brain function of physical stress from heart and blood vessel disease, cancer, and chronic pain. But there is no question that emotional stress can also produce a substantial change in brain function, with a loss of brain efficiency. Recent studies also point to stress as having a major influence on the efficiency and strength of our immune system.

The brain has enormous power to affect the well-being and health of the entire body. A healthy brain is a force toward maintaining a healthy body. A stressed, unhappy, and depressed brain makes the body and its defenses more vulnerable. Notice how often the loss of a lifelong spouse causes the surviving partner to become seriously or serially ill or the death of one partner in a long and successful marriage will be followed quickly by the death of the other.

Not only does the death of a loved one cause emotional stress that may affect health, but work-related stress can have the same result, with the production of a profound depression and resulting impairment of attention, concentration, and recent memory. That was the case with Harry, a fifty-six-year-old Englishman who had come to America as a securities salesman and now worked for a major brokerage firm. A charming, astute, and persistent salesman, his successful record in the mutual fund business caused him to be promoted to the branch managership of the company. Then his firm was rocked by financial scandals, and it had to lay off a number of employees. Harry was relegated to a minor position in the company and was in danger of losing both his job and his ability to support his family.

Because of his previous financial success, he had bought a large home and his children were all in private schools. Suddenly, he was faced not only with the prospect of a reduced income but with the possibility of no income at all. People who had openly admired his skill and persistence began openly criticizing him in public and, worse, many just ignored him. He became susceptible to repeated bouts of the flu, and in a short period of time he suffered a lower back strain and a urinary tract infection.

Harry became severely depressed and started to drink alcohol excessively. He was put on antidepressant medication and his medical and hospital expenses further taxed his financial resources. His depression became so severe that he even contemplated electroshock treatment. Then one night he went to church services conducted by a minister who also happened to be a very effective psychotherapist. Harry was so impressed by the sermon that he went up afterward to talk to the minister, who took him into his rectory for some counseling.

The minister tried to instill in Harry a new concept — at least new to Harry — giving him the belief that there was something in the world that was more important than his financial crisis. It was called religious faith.

Harry later told me that it was like getting a shot of penicillin for an infection or having a broken leg heal. Suddenly the stress that caused him to be so depressed dissipated and he was able to work for the first time in many months. He gained mastery over his own emotions and body functions and felt a sense of well-being.

He realized then that he wasn't the cause of his company's failure or scandals. He had established a reputation for hard work, honesty, and integrity, and with those skills he started life over and went into a new business in southern California. Harry became more successful than he ever was before and attained a measure of security that reinforced his own feelings of good health and self-confidence.

Part III

A Complete Program for Building and Rebuilding Brain Power Energy

Chapter 9

Nutrition
and the Brain

RESTRUCTURING YOUR NUTRITIONAL LIFE

When I tell some of my patients that my review of their diet and nutrition indicates that they are going to have to restructure their lives, I often get the reply "I don't think I can stick to a diet program very well. I just don't have the will power and, besides, life is too short not to live dangerously once in a while." When I hear words to that effect, I know that I'm talking with a hardened veteran of the diet wars.

After years of fighting the losing battle against excessive eating, most people become cynical about the whole process and think negatively about their ability to control their own weight. What these people don't realize, and what I can't stress enough, is that the very foods they eat cause them to lose control over their eating habits. In effect, they can't win the diet wars because they're using their weapons against themselves.

Recently a young woman named Katie came into my office holding a copy of a popular diet book. She said to me, "Doctor, I've been on this diet now for two months. I've lost twelve pounds, but I feel lousy and have terrible headaches all the time. In fact, the same thing happens to me whenever I go on a diet. I think my body's trying to tell me that it doesn't want to be thin.''

After I ruled out any sort of neurological cause for her headaches, I began to take a detailed inventory of the foods she was eating on her diets. I found that not only was her diet deficient in a number of key vitamins and minerals, but some of the foods she consumed might be the cause of allergic reactions. I suggested that she eliminate some of the dairy products she was consuming, as a starting point, and then go through the same elimination procedure for two or three other food categories if she found no improvement after that first step.

Two weeks later I got a call from Katie telling me her headaches were gone. It wasn't that her body didn't want to be thin, it was that her body was allergic to two specific dairy foods she had been eating. "Now that you've figured out which foods cause your mind and body to rebel," I said, "isn't it time to give yourself the nutrients that will help you to become stronger?" "I can't eat three meals a day," she said. "I'm still thirty-five pounds overweight." To which I replied, "You don't need to eat a lot to get proper nutrition. In fact, if you take in the nutrients that help your brain work at peak efficiency, your brain will actually help you stick to a weight loss diet.''

Virtually every program that tells people how to lose weight is based on two simple components: eating less and exercising more. Except in unusual circumstances, people who want to lose weight accomplish that goal by doing both those things. But if it is really that simple, why is it so hard to lose weight?

The reason is that the homeostatic weight control mechanism is located in the brain and is controlled by complex chemical messages. The message your stomach sends to your brain telling it that you're hungry is a very powerful message, one that is not easily ignored. Our brains don't have separate monitoring systems to calculate the number of calories that have been consumed and to allow them to automatically turn off hunger pangs when the optimal number is reached. Instead, we must rely on the thinking, rational, and intellectual parts of our brains to regulate food intake. When those functions are impaired or are not working at peak efficiency, we run into problems.

For most of us, nutrition is a hit-or-miss proposition. We are bombarded with messages from companies telling us why their food is more fun or glamorous, our eating schedules change constantly depending on the vagaries of everyday life, and we don't get enough solid information in an easily understandable form that would allow us to be more selective in choosing the foods we eat. When we do actually get the "three square meals per day" that doctors have been talking about for decades, we're apt to end up eating too many calories while still missing out on some of the essential nutrients our brains and bodies need. Often we just fall into patterns of eating lots of foods that, taken as a whole, are bad for us.

A short time ago, I was waiting in a supermarket check-out line when I noticed that the man in front of me was a patient named Doug who had come to see me about a year before. Doug, a sixty-two-year-old retired shipbuilder and ironworker, was seventy-five pounds overweight and looked to be in terrible physical condition. He had already had one heart attack and one small stroke. Also, he had neglected his dental hygiene to the point where he had almost no teeth. One look at his shopping cart told me all the reasons he was deteriorating so rapidly. Next to an enormous bag of potato chips were packages of all-pork frankfurters and processed bologna. And next to them were several jars of baby food and a half gallon of chocolate ice cream. I also couldn't help noticing the large bottle of antacid tucked away in the corner of the cart. It wasn't as if Doug couldn't afford to buy good food or as if he didn't have time to prepare healthful meals; it was just that he had accustomed himself to eating high-calorie foods containing large amounts of salt and fat. I wasn't surprised that he was overweight as much as I was surprised that he was only seventy-five pounds overweight.

The reason weight loss diets often don't work is that you can't stick to them, and the reason you can't stick to them is that you're trying to change the *quantity* of the food you eat without changing the *quality* of the nutrition your brain is getting. You can't expect your brain to respond positively to a reduced calorie intake when you insist on depriving it of the nutrients it needs to function properly. Once you learn what your body needs and how to get it, you'll be able to take a sensible approach to controlling your weight.

In this chapter I present some basic information about nutrition, with a special emphasis on nutrition and the brain, that will help you remember which vitamins, minerals, nutrients, and amino acids are necessary for optimal brain function. Chapter 10 contains an easy-to-read chart that summarizes the daily amounts you need of each for a healthy body and a healthy brain.

VITAMINS

Vitamins are substances that your body does not produce but that are nevertheless essential to normal functioning. People who don't know much about nutrition frequently ask me, "How do I know whether I'm getting enough vitamins? I don't even know which foods contain which vitamins." If you don't have time to research vitamin content, the best way to educate yourself is to consistently read the labels on the packages of foods you buy. With improved labeling, it is now possible to know the exact vitamin content of such products as cereals, breads, and canned goods. Still, that leaves all the fresh fruits, vegetables, meats, and poultry products, to name just a few, on which the vitamin content is not listed. I present some of the basic information here, but to find out precise amounts you can consult one of the many books giving nutritional content of foods.

Some time ago, nutritionists realized that there were minimum amounts of vitamins and other nutrients that everyone needed to function in a disease-free state. By 1958, the U.S. Food and Drug Administration (FDA) established daily amounts for food labeling purposes, called Minimum Daily Requirements, which were felt to be adequate to prevent deficiencies in most people. It became clear that the minimums were too low, so in 1973 the FDA introduced a new system of nutrition labeling called U.S. RDA standards (U.S. Recommended Daily Allowances), which replaced minimums with slightly higher amounts. At about the same time, the National Academy of Sciences– National Research Council began to generate lists of vitamins known as Recommended Daily Dietary Allowances, which were nearly the same as the government's standards but were somewhat more precise in terms of age and sex. (See Table 2.)

Table 2

ADULT DIETARY ALLOWANCE STANDARDS FOR
SELECTED VITAMINS AND MINERALS

	Minimum Daily Requirements (1958)*	U. S. Recommended Daily Allowances (1973)**	Recommended Daily Dietary Allowances (1980)†
Calcium	750 mg	1000 mg	800 mg
Iron	10.0 mg	18.0 mg	18.0 mg
Thiamine	1.0 mg	1.5 mg	1.4 mg
Riboflavin	1.2 mg	1.7 mg	1.6 mg
Niacin	10.0 mg	20.0 mg	18.0 mg
Vitamin C	30.0 mg	60.0 mg	60.0 mg

*Source: Title 21, Code of Federal Regulations, and 21 CFR, 1959 supplement. Figures used from column labeled "Adults."

**Source: U.S. Recommended Daily Allowances for Labeling Purposes, 1973 Food and Drug Administration. Figures used from column labeled "Adults and Children 4 or More Years of Age."

†Source: Food and Nutrition Board, National Academy of Sciences–National Research Council, Recommended Daily Dietary Allowances, Revised 1980. Figures used from highest value for either males age 23–50 or females age 23–50.

I'm a strong supporter of RDAs and U.S. RDAs, and I think that in making this information widely available we have prevented many millions of serious illnesses. The problem is that if you take the RDAs of all the essential vitamins, you'll be getting close to the minimum requirement of each. But the *minimum* required amount of some vitamins is not anywhere near what I consider an *optimal* amount. Instead of looking at the nutritional content on a cereal box over breakfast and thinking that you're home free for the day because it says "100% of the U.S. RDA" beside each vitamin, you have to understand that getting 100 percent means that you're just scraping by. Many people make a great fuss about getting RDAs until I tell them that it's like looking at your school report card with all Ds on it and saying, "Look how well I did; I didn't flunk a single course."

Rather than thinking in terms of minimums or RDAs, I want you to think in terms of optimums. If you take in the recommended amount of vitamin C, for example, you will avoid getting a disease known as scurvy, in which the gums bleed and become swollen and the body's connective tissue does not regenerate properly. However, it's my impression that some patients who get only the recommended daily allowance of vitamin C still have vague deficiency symptoms such as a loss of motivation or a mild depression. These symptoms, of course, are magnified many times in scurvy. Doctors aren't usually trained to think in terms of a vitamin deficiency when they hear of symptoms such as these, but some of my patients with these symptoms were able to reverse their symptoms by doing something as simple as drinking more freshly squeezed orange juice (a good source of vitamin C).

MAJOR B VITAMIN DEFICIENCIES AND BRAIN DISEASE

Of all the vitamins, those that are most important to optimal brain function are the B vitamins. B vitamins are water-soluble, which means that for the most part they're not stored in the body for long and consequently you need to replenish your supply of them frequently. There are seven B vitamins, four of which are quite important for optimal brain function. If you don't get those four in a sufficient amount, a profound disease of the brain will result.

The first of these is vitamin B_{12}. A lack of folate and this vitamin produces a disease called pernicious anemia, in which there is an increase in the size of the red blood cells.* Pernicious anemia affects the brain indirectly by reducing the number of red blood cells that transport oxygen. It also affects the brain directly because without this vitamin a degenerative disease of the spinal cord occurs that causes an individual to lose the sensation of where his or her limbs are in space and also causes a profound muscle weakness in which the muscles may become very spastic. Physicians call this disease combined degeneration of the spinal cord, and it also produces a severe disturbance in brain function. I've seen patients with clinical symptoms ranging all the way from irritability, apathy, somnolence, and suspiciousness to severe emotional instability. They may even develop a marked confusional or depressive psychotic state, which eventually produces profound intellectual deterioration.

Biochemically, vitamin B_{12} plays an important role in the formation of the myelin sheath around nerve fibers, both peripherally and in the brain and spinal cord. The vitamin is not found in any vegetables, so I keep that fact in mind whenever I examine vegetarians who do not take vitamin supplements. Quite often, in fact, I've had doctors refer patients to me for sophisticated diagnostic tests to determine the cause of memory problems, depression, or fatigue (to name just a few symptoms), when the doctors failed to do a simple blood test that would have revealed the problem.

The second important vitamin in this category is B_1 (thia-

---

*The blood disorder in pernicious anemia can be corrected by adequate amounts of folate, but vitamin B_{12} is necessary to reverse the associated changes in the spinal cord and brain.

mine). A deficiency in vitamin B_1 produces, in mild cases, a disease called beriberi, which is often associated with degeneration of the peripheral nerves and numbness of the hands and feet. It is also directly related in more extreme cases to a brain disease in chronic alcoholics called Wernicke's Korsakoff syndrome. In severe deficiency states victims develop an abnormality of eyeball movements. This is often followed by a disabling memory loss and is related to a brain abnormality in the inner part of the thalamus. Depending on how early the disease is recognized, some or many of the symptoms may be reversed by giving the patient vitamin B_1, but unfortunately this does not always occur.

Vitamin B_3 (which may take the form of niacin) also has a profound effect on brain function. A deficiency in this vitamin produces the mental symptoms of dementia in a disease called pellagra. Around the turn of the century, two common diseases caused many patients to be committed to mental hospitals: pellagra and syphilis of the brain. At that time, these patients looked just like the other patients, who were either psychotic or demented. Now both of these diseases are completely treatable, and they are no longer in the province of psychiatry but are included in the category of general medicine.

An additional fact about vitamin B_3 is that it has a closely related chemical compound called tryptophan, an amino acid that is essential for normal brain function. Tryptophan, in turn, is related to the production of serotonin, an important neurotransmitter in the brain that is the focus of considerable controversy regarding nutritional therapy for emotional and brain disorders (discussed in more detail later in this chapter).

The last vitamin of the most important B vitamins is vitamin B_6, which is also called pyridoxine. There is increasing evidence that vitamin B_6 is intimately connected with metabolism of the brain, especially in infants. Low vitamin B_6 intake can be associated with a syndrome of hyperirritability, gastrointestinal distress, and increased startle responses. It can also produce epileptic seizures and an epileptic pattern on a brain wave test.

These four B vitamins are the most important vitamins for healthy brain function. It's not that vitamins A, B$_2$, B$_5$, B$_9$, C, D, E, and H are not important. They are important, but they are not as directly related to brain function as the four B vitamins. In Chapter 10 I recommend optimal daily allowances for vitamins, and I encourage you to follow those guidelines for all the vitamins, not just the four essential B vitamins.

MINERALS AND THE BRAIN

I once treated a young boy who, among other problems, had a severe iron deficiency. I explained to him that iron is both an element and a mineral that is found in the earth and that the body needs it in very small amounts. He asked me, "If you only need a little, then why did I get sick?" I said, "A little goes a long way, but you didn't get any."

If you don't get any minerals, you'll be in somewhat dire straits (although it's difficult to get no minerals). You need a couple dozen minerals, including iron, zinc, copper, and iodine, but because they are so plentiful in foods, except in a few countries, it's difficult to become deficient in any of them except iron and iodine. Minerals are incorporated into the body's enzyme systems and are important in maintaining the normal regulatory mechanisms and metabolism of the body, which ensure that the brain is continually presented with the correct amount of oxygen and carbon dioxide, energy foods, proteins (and their building blocks, amino acids), ions, and trace elements. In this category, trace minerals play an important part in supporting brain function.

Even when the heart and lungs are working normally, there may not be enough oxygen presented to the brain if the red blood cell count is too low. The same holds true if the hemoglobin fraction in the blood is reduced or if iron, which is essential for oxygen transport, is deficient in amount. An iron deficiency anemia can quickly be corrected by supplementing the diet with iron compounds, although you have to be very careful not to overload your body with iron. This can be done inadvertently by drinking some types of wine. Although most wines contain less than 10 milligrams of iron per liter, some wines contain more than 40 milligrams per liter, and this may lead to iron overload, which in turn can produce a hard-to-treat liver disease. Iron deficiency anemia is most common in menstruating woman whose diet is inadequate to replace the iron they lose in their menstrual blood.

Zinc deficiency is very rarely responsible for clinical disease, but its relation to brain disease has been suggested by the Australian scientist F. M. Burnett, who thinks that the deficiency may be related to the early development of Alzheimer's disease. That supplementary zinc can prevent or delay the onset of the dementing symptoms in people who are genetically at risk for this syndrome has not yet been proved, but I and many other scientists are eager to see the clinical data that proponents of this theory have.

ELECTROLYTES AND THE BRAIN

An electrolyte is a substance that, in a solution such as blood, dissociates into ions and in so doing conducts a small electric charge. Ions are particles having either a positive or a negative charge; they are found inside and outside the membranes of nerve cells and fibers, and they help control the excitability of nerve elements. The concentration of the ions within and around nerve cells is related to the concentration of ions in the serum of the blood that circulates to and from the brain.

The serum level of essential ions such as sodium, potassium, chloride, calcium, magnesium, and carbonate has to be kept within a very narrow normal range to avoid symptoms of brain dysfunction. This is especially true of calcium. If someone is given excessive amounts of calcium to correct a low serum calcium (as in the condition known as tetany), the calcium ion concentration in the blood becomes elevated, which results in mental changes. At small elevations of calcium, slight changes in behavior may be noticeable, but higher dosages can cause stupor and even coma.

One woman named Jane was brought into Boston City Hospital, having been forcibly removed from another hospital where she had created a continuing disturbance. The doctors at her former hospital thought she had a psychiatric problem, and since she had run out of money to pay for the treatment of her disabling illness, they sent her to Boston City Hospital as a charity case. When we checked her blood calcium we found it to be abnormally high. This resulted from a cancer that had spread to many of her bones. As the bones degenerated, the level of calcium in her bloodstream increased. When we corrected the abnormally high calcium level, her psychiatric symptoms disappeared.

The concentration of sodium ions in the blood is related to the hydration level in the body. A low serum sodium is often related to overhydration, which may occur, especially in hot weather, if large quantities of water are drunk to quench thirst while sodium is lost in excessive perspiration. Overhydration can also occur in overenthusiastic beer drinkers and produces some swelling of tissues and even swelling of the brain. The mental consequences of overhydration or low sodium are somewhat nonspecific. In the early stages, the victim will have difficulty concentrating and may become drowsy and even giddy. The brain swelling may cause headache and nausea. If the condition goes unchecked, confusion may occur, with behavioral disturbances and even convulsions and coma.

In dehydration, a depletion of body water, the serum sodium may become very elevated. Dehydration may produce shrinkage in the brain, with irritability, overbreathing, and fever. If left untreated, it also leads to mental changes and even stupor.

Elderly people in whom the body's regulatory mechanisms are deficient may be susceptible to both dehydration and overhydration. It is not uncommon to find nursing home patients without sufficient water to replenish their needs on a hot day. I've done mental status exams on these patients and found that within a period of three or four hours they may develop signs of intellectual deterioration including loss of recent memory, disorientation to time, and inability to find words. These abnormalities are reversed when the proper amounts of water and salt are given. It is important, however, not to try to correct these kinds of imbalances too quickly, particularly in an elderly individual. The corrections must be carried out gradually over several days or damage to the brainstem can occur.

CLASSICAL VERSUS MODERN THEORIES OF BRAIN NUTRITION

We have so far discussed nutritional disorders and deficiencies that are related to specific vitamins, minerals, or electrolytes. Many classical nutritionists limit the relation between brain disease and nutrition to minimum doses of those elements. They claim that you need only enough of the essential vitamins so that disease states do not occur. Having an excess amount of vitamins is unnecessary, they claim, and taking much more than the recommended daily allowances may have adverse consequences.

However, I know of at least twenty-five disorders or diseases in humans that respond to doses of vitamins that are ten to one hundred times greater than the recommended normal dietary intake. In such a disorder, the consequences of a genetic defect in an enzyme system, for example, may be prevented by a high concentration of a vitamin. The benefit of megavitamin therapy in these disorders is well established.

Besides being critical of megavitamin therapies in certain cases, most orthodox nutritionists feel that if you've taken in enough protein energy foods, if you are not suffering from a vitamin deficiency, and if your blood sugar and other electrolytes and metabolites are at normal levels, your behavior and brain function are not going to be influenced by your diet. In other words, they say that there is an optimal level of protein, sugar, electrolytes, minerals, and vitamins — that is, a level that prevents deficiency states — and added nutrients or vitamins will not improve brain function. Not all doctors, including me, believe this. A group of researchers at the Massachusetts Institute of Technology headed by Richard and Judith Wurtman have held international seminars on the relations between nutrition and brain function and behavior. Presentations at these seminars sometimes confirmed and sometimes disputed conventional wisdom.

Those researchers are not the only ones who have cast some doubt on the views of the traditional nutritionists. In a January 1988 issue of the British medical journal *The Lancet*, D. Benton and G. Roberts reported on the effects of a vitamin and mineral supplement on the intelligence quotients of a group of English schoolchildren. Ninety children, aged twelve and thirteen, kept a dietary diary before the study started. In most cases the average intake of vitamins was close to the recommended daily allowance, although for a small minority the intake was low. The recommended daily allowance was less commonly met for minerals.

A multivitamin/mineral supplement or a placebo was administered in a scientifically controlled study to sixty of the children for eight months. The remaining thirty children, the control group, took neither supplement nor placebo. The supplement group, but not the placebo group or the control group, showed a significant increase in nonverbal intelligence.

Also in 1988, Dr. Steven Schoenthaler, a California criminologist, advanced the theory that improving the diet of juvenile delinquents reduced their levels of antisocial behavior. Starting in 1987, he performed an experiment on inmates in a top-security prison in Oklahoma, following the experimental method that scientists use in the trials of new drugs. Although prison officials viewed Schoenthaler's theories unfavorably, according to reporter Tony Edwards, they agreed to let him do a three-month trial. During this time, half the inmates, chosen at random, were fed a daily vitamin and mineral supplement and the other half were given a placebo. At the end of the trial the examiners found a substantial reduction in offenses even among the inmates not on vitamins. However, the skeptical prison officials were astonished to find that the group that took the vitamins had an even more marked improvement in their behavior: a 27 percent greater reduction in offenses than the control group. Schoenthaler concluded that a subset of the criminal population, estimated at 30 percent, has brain-altered function disorders because of poor nutrition. In these people, a dramatic improvement in behavior can occur in just a few days, according to Schoenthaler, if proper nutritional guidelines are followed.

Another example of the danger of setting a low standard for vitamins that will avoid obvious disease but may not give the opportunity for optimal brain function was illustrated by the experiments of R. F. Harrell. She pointed out that many nutritionists consider a maintenance dose of between 1.0 and 1.3 milligrams of thiamine (vitamin B_1) per day to be adequate for nutrition. In the 1940s, Harrell studied eleven-year-old children in an American orphanage who ate the same daily menu that supplied about 1.0 milligram of thiamine a day. In an experiment, a thiamine supplement was supplied in a scientifically controlled study for a period of several years. Harrell found that those who received the thiamine supplement had significant improvement in intelligence, visual acuity, and memory and a decrease in reaction times compared with children who were given placebos.

One of the difficulties in evaluating the effects of added protein, energy foods, and vitamins on brain function and human behavior is that testing is often carried out in patients who have obvious brain disease. For example, megavitamin therapies have been tested in patients with schizophrenia, and a whole branch of psychiatry, known as orthomolecular psychiatry, is devoted to treating schizophrenic patients with huge doses of vitamins.

In a similar fashion, dietary supplements of choline or lecithin or drugs that increase the amount of acetylcholine in the memory circuits of the temporal lobe have been given to people with Alzheimer's. The rationale is that Alzheimer patients' failing memories are probably due to an acetylcholine deficiency in the inner parts of the temporal lobes. Research scientists administered the supplementary choline in an attempt to improve memory function in these people. Does the lack of a striking therapeutic effect of the nutrient choline in patients with Alzheimer's disease mean that the use of choline supplements in the diet of normal people is ineffective? No, it does not.

A study done by Dr. Natraj Sitaram and co-workers from the National Institutes of Health, for example, showed that a dietary addition of 10 grams of choline a day did have an obvious effect on some components of memory in a scientifically controlled study in normal subjects. Two different tests were used to study the effects on learning and memory in normal volunteers whose average age was twenty-four. The first was an uncategorized serial learning test, and the second was a selective reminding test. In both tests, the effect of choline on memory was statistically significant. In the first test, the subjects took fewer trials to learn a list of ten unrelated words, and under the effects of choline the poorer performers showed greater improvement than the good performers.

In the first trial of the selective reminding tests, a twelve-word list of common English words was read, "half of which were high imagery words such as 'chair,' and half of which were low imagery words such as 'lie.' " On successive trials the only words read were those not correctly recalled on the previous trial. Learning and recall were repeated until the subjects said all twelve words perfectly on two successive trials or until the trials had been done twelve times.

The results showed that choline improved the storage and recall only of low-imagery words. This was partially due to the improved consistency of recall from trial to trial. As stated in the results, "Words recalled correctly on one trial were more likely to be recalled correctly on the next trial if they followed the administration of choline rather than a placebo."

This kind of research, which has been verified in other laboratories, is important because it contradicts the prevailing ideas about dietary supplementation. Choline, for example, is partially synthesized within the body. However, it has been proved in human beings that the consumption of added lecithin or choline increases the choline levels in the blood and in the spinal fluid. It is possible, although as yet unproved, that this also increases the release of acetylcholine in the brain. There is, however, no question that dietary choline as a supplement produces an improvement in certain kinds of memory performance in young people. This may be the result of vitaminlike actions of choline rather than a direct effect on acetylcholine concentrations.*

When choline supplements were used in elderly individuals who had significant problems with memory, they did not produce a marked improvement, except in one study. The exact conditions of the elderly patients tested in these studies were not clear, so it is quite possible that enough of them had brain disease so that the effects of choline were blunted. One study did find marked improvement in memory functions in 60 percent of elderly patients tested, an encouraging result. It has also been shown recently that even in patients with Alzheimer's disease, the increase in concentration of acetylcholine in the memory cir-

---

*I recently spoke to Dr. Sitaram about his study and he alluded to the fact that the choline effect may be related to vitamin or cell membrane functions of the choline. Other researchers are more inclined to attribute the memory response to a change in acetylcholine concentrations.

cuit of the brain produced a temporary improvement in recall memory when this was accomplished with a medication called physostigmine.

Three other neurotransmitters in the brain affect activity and aggression, the perception of sensation, sleep, mood, and performance. The three are norepinephrine, dopamine, and serotonin. Their concentration in the brain can be affected by the intake of certain amino acids, including tryptophan and tyrosine, which are contained in food. It is increasingly clear from research that brain messages passed from cell to cell by neurotransmitters can be enhanced by the food we eat. The neurotransmitter dopamine, for example, which is deficient in the brains of patients with Parkinson's disease, and the neurotransmitter norepinephrine are considered to be the alertness chemicals. Increased levels of these neurotransmitters produce distinct changes in mood and behavior, including a tendency to think more quickly and react more rapidly.

Experiments indicate that more study is needed into the explanations for the brain mechanisms involved in the effects of certain foods on the brain. My own studies in experimental animals allowed me to inject norepinephrine, dopamine, or serotonin into selected areas of the brain without damaging surrounding brain tissue while the animals were awake. I found that injecting norepinephrine into the part of the emotional brain that controls emotional behavior did not produce an alerting response. In rage animals it produced a calming. When I injected norepinephrine into the regulatory centers of a monkey's brain it produced taming, not excitement. When I injected norepinephrine into the pain centers of a monkey, it produced an increased threshold for pain. Serotonin produced a decreased threshold for pain. Thus it comes as no surprise to me that when people eat foods containing large amounts of certain amino acids, their mood and behavior will be affected.

The effects that the Wurtmans and other brain researchers have observed about various dietary substances are real. They have reported on research that shows that high-protein, low-fat foods increase alertness and concentration, while a meal high in carbo- hydrates is associated with relaxation. Their work is at the cut- ting edge of new and important research on the relation between food, brain function, feelings, and behavior. While we know that certain foods trigger certain brain responses, we are still at an early stage in our understanding of the biochemical mech- anisms involved. For you, however, it's not so important to know how these mechanisms work, but that they *do* work.

Our increasing knowledge of the actual consequences of eat- ing a particular food alone or in combination with other foods has allowed us to select certain kinds of diets that can enhance certain of our abilities, change some of our behavior at appro- priate times, and improve our efficiency. I have developed a diet, not as a weight loss plan but as a way to increase brain function. It's called the brain power diet. Chapters 10 and 11 describe this new eating plan in detail.

Chapter 10

The Brain
Power Diet

GENERAL GUIDELINES

Certain general principles are applied to all diets, whether the diets are for weight loss, controlling certain metabolites, or improving brain function, and my diet is no exception. One general principle, for example, is not to take in excessive amounts of salt because in some people it tends to produce a chronic increase in blood pressure and increases the risk of stroke. The same is true for ingesting hard or saturated fats. A diet containing a substantial amount of saturated fat accelerates the process of atherosclerosis, or internal hardening of the arteries, which in turn increases the chance of stroke or brain hemorrhage.

The brain power diet is not specifically intended to help you gain or lose weight, although it can be used for both by simply regulating food portions and adjusting your activity level. But I must caution you against both sharp gains and sharp losses in weight. An increase in body weight followed by a reduced-calorie diet in which your body lives off its own hard fats is a prescription for hardening of the arteries, heart attack, or stroke.

If you're really serious about maintaining your weight or losing weight, I encourage you to follow the advice I always give my patients when I put them on any kind of diet: You must weigh yourself daily on a *doctor's* scale. Doctor's scales are the kind with movable weights, the ones that you can't cheat on by jiggling back and forth on the springs. They're expensive (about $200), but they're worth every penny. If you weigh yourself at the same time of the day, first thing in the morning, the scale will tell you how many calories you can consume or how much liquid you can drink.

Sometimes I hear someone tell me, "Well, doctor, I don't need to weigh myself. I'll know if I'm gaining weight." Unfortunately, most people who gain weight are the last ones to know. It isn't until their abdomens start bulging over their belts or their dress size increases by two or three or someone remarks on their weight that they realize they're getting out of shape. By that time, it's much too late to take quick, effective measures that will avoid the metabolizing of their own hard body fats to get down to the weight category in which they belong.

Generally, the body is a heat machine. Calories taken in have to be balanced by calories used. Unused calories are stored as complex carbohydrates — or fat. Various factors, such as absorption of nutrients from the gut, metabolic rate, and hormonal levels, may govern this process, and that's why some people put on weight more easily than others. Fluid retention is another factor that may alter body weight. People who retain water in their tissues have a more difficult time achieving the proper weight than those who do not. This, in turn, may depend on normal heart and kidney function.

In addition to what I've just mentioned, people have differing caloric needs, depending on their sex and age. Men, who are usually a little larger, require a slightly greater daily caloric intake until the age of twenty-two (between 2500 and 3300 calories), with a gradual reduction to age fifty, and then a more substantial decline after age fifty-two (to between 2000 and 2600 calories). Women require 600 to 800 fewer calories per day than men of the same age category.

It is important in this diet, as in any diet, to have foods and beverages that you like and will consume. Diets should not be punitive, for eating is one of the joys of life. Our aim is to make it into a long-term joy rather than a series of short-term binges with unacceptable diet alterations in between.

It may help to keep in mind a few things about taste and food enjoyment. First, the taste of food is limited to four elements: sweet, sour, bitter, and salt. All of the other flavors of food and drink are related to odor, not taste. The most delightful odors are usually retained in fat or lipid material. If you use different kinds of spices or the residue of flaming wines or liqueurs (with the alcohol burned off) to impart taste, you can make up for some of the odors that linger with old-fashioned high-fat diets.

Second, the stomach is essentially just a distensible bag. It is somewhat elastic, but if it is distended too much it will assume a chronically dilated form. That means that if it is not kept filled up at its new, expanded capacity, you will notice feelings of hunger and will have to keep eating or drinking just to keep your stomach filled. At that point, it will not be a matter of eating to satisfy your real hunger requirements but eating to prevent the hunger pangs of an overstuffed, dilated stomach.

Don't become a slave to your taste buds or stomach. You are in control of what you eat, and there are ways to satisfy food taste and quantity desires without resorting to eating a lot of empty calories with no nutritional value.

PRINCIPLES OF COMBINING FOODS
FOR OPTIMAL BRAIN POWER

Everything I say about the brain power diet is based on your getting the correct amounts of electrolytes, vitamins, minerals, and amino acids in your daily diet. Many doctors who prescribe diets for their patients take special care to say that you should follow the diet to the letter so that you won't have to take vitamin supplements. Such statements have often puzzled me because the supplements in bottles are just as good for the body as the vitamins, minerals, and other nutrients found in food.

It's often difficult for people to follow special diets, not only because it takes a long time to prepare the foods but because it takes time to shop for the groceries and find all the ingredients. In other cases, people may have food preferences that are not included in their doctor's diet, and they may not know how to substitute one food for another.

I've developed what I consider an exciting range of dishes and foods that, if eaten conscientiously, will provide you with your basic nutritional needs. You would, however, have to eat far more of each of the foods than is healthy for you to get the optimal amounts of vitamins and nutrients for brain power. Therefore, along with the menus in Chapter 11, I've included the amounts of vitamins you should take as supplements because they are not present in sufficient amounts in the foods. I list all the nutrients you need and their correct amounts here, but you really don't need to worry about supplementing more than a few if you eat the basic diet I outline.

The key nutrients associated with brain function are the electrolytes: calcium, magnesium, sodium, potassium, and chloride; and the vitamins: B_1 (thiamine), B_3 (niacin), B_6 (pyridoxine), B_9 (folate), B_{12}, and C; as well as minerals: iron, copper, and zinc. Essential brain nutrients also include choline, which is an important metabolite, although it cannot be classified as a vitamin since it is partially synthesized within the body. Furthermore, the quantities of choline required by the human body are considerably larger than those of most substances considered to be vitamins. Essential amino acids, especially tyrosine and tryptophan, which contain chemical building blocks of neurotransmitters and the building blocks of protein, also have an effect on human behavior and brain function.

Other elements such as iodine, which may have a profound effect on the brain of the developing fetus, should be included in a diet for expectant mothers who live in an area of endemic goiter

Table 3

	Minimum	Optimal
Vitamins		
Vitamin A	5000 IU**	5000 IU
Vitamin D	400 IU	400 IU
Vitamin E	30 IU	30 IU
Vitamin C	60.0 mg	1000.0 mg
Vitamin B$_1$ (thiamine)	1.5 mg	20.0 mg
Vitamin B$_2$ (riboflavin)	1.7 mg	10.0 mg
Vitamin B$_3$ (niacin)	20.0 mg	250.0 mg
Vitamin B$_5$ (pantothenic acid)	10.0 mg	20.0 mg
Vitamin B$_6$ (pyridoxine)	2.0 mg	20.0 mg
Vitamin B$_9$ (folate)	0.4 mg	1.0 mg
Vitamin B$_{12}$ (cobalamines)	6.0 mcg	100.0 mcg
Vitamin H† (biotin)	N/A	200.0 mcg
Choline‡	N/A	3.0 g
Minerals		
Calcium§	1.0 g	1.6 g
Phosphorus§	1.0 g	1.6 g
Iodine	150.0 mcg	150.0 mcg
Iron	18.0 mg	20.0 mg
Magnesium	400.0 mg	400.0 mg
Copper	2.0 mg	3.0 mg
Zinc	15.0 mg	25.0 mg
Other		
Spring water	N/A	1.5–2.0 liters (45–60 oz.)

*For people who do not have allergies to specific foods containing these vitamins and for people who don't have diabetes or liver, thyroid, or kidney disease. Vitamin or nutritional supplements may be necessary for people who have an allergy or intolerance to certain basic foods like milk, cheese, nuts, or fish. Nonallergenic food supplements are available and are strongly recommended to overcome the potential nutritional deficiencies that would otherwise occur in people intolerant to basic foods.

**IU stands for international units, an international standard for measuring quantities of substances such as vitamins.

†Various amounts of this vitamin are normally produced in the intestine.

‡Many nutritionists do not consider choline to be a vitamin because some amount of it is produced in the body, but I consider it so important that you may need to supplement it.

§You may substitute 3.2 grams per day of calcium phosphate.

Note: See p. 240 for additional information on vitamin and mineral supplements.

such as a mountainous region. The use of iodized salt in normal amounts is sufficient. Other vitamins, such as vitamins D, B_2 (riboflavin), and B_5 (pantothenic acid), have indirect influences on brain function, so they too are considered part of the diet. These essential vitamins, minerals, nutrients, amino acids, and the metabolite choline should be included in at least one meal every day.

Table 3 summarizes all the key nutrients you need in their optimal amounts. It is important to ingest at least the amounts listed. If necessary (and it usually is), this can be accomplished with supplemental nutrients or vitamins, which you can purchase in individual packages from your pharmacist or health food store. Also, I have made arrangements with Pharmacaps, Inc., and Schiff, two vitamin manufacturers, to have these supplemental amounts contained in just three capsules, one to be taken with each meal.* The supplements are available in most health food stores. Be careful to take only the suggested amounts to avoid any side effects.

Using good judgment is essential whenever you take dietary supplements. The amounts I recommend here should serve as a guide for you. Circumstances may cause you to deviate from the optimal levels, but at least you will have a good idea of whether you're getting too much or too little of any specific vitamin. I do encourage you, however, to try getting as close to the optimal amounts as you can.

AMINO ACIDS

The building blocks of proteins are amino acids. Not all amino acids are equal or produce the same effect on brain function.

---

*The Schiff product does not contain choline. The Pharmacaps product contains concentrated choline in a form that doesn't impart a fishy odor. A number of other vitamin and mineral products are available in pharmacies and natural-food stores.

Table 4

FOODS CONTAINING LARGE CONCENTRATIONS
OF TRYPTOPHAN AND TYROSINE

Food	Tyrosine	Tryptophan
Soy flour		•
Dry skim milk	•	•
Cheddar cheese	•	•
Parmesan cheese	•	•
Eggs	•	•
Roast sirloin	•	•
Roast chicken	•	•
Roast pheasant	•	•
Corned beef	•	•
Peanut butter		•

Tryptophan and tyrosine are among the most important amino acids for changing brain function. Tyrosine is related to an increased ability to concentrate. This amino acid is found in negligible amounts in almost all fruits and most vegetables, with the exception of kidney beans. In contrast, poultry, some fish, and some red meats contain substantial amounts of tyrosine.

Dietary tryptophan produces relaxation and drowsiness. Although many meats contain substantial amounts of tryptophan, they will not cause drowsiness when they are ingested because of competing mechanisms that enhance the preferential absorption of other amino acids during a protein meal. However, certain sources of vegetable protein that may be part of a carbohydrate meal may contain substantial amounts of tryptophan. One of these sources is soybean flour, especially defatted soybean flour, which is also one of the best sources of dietary choline. A high-carbohydrate/low-protein meal will call forth more insulin from the pancreas, reducing the concentration of competing amino acids and allowing the concentration of tryptophan to rise. This produces a relaxing effect on behavior and is a useful meal before retiring.

As you can see, it's useful to know which amino acids are contained in which foods if you want to make them work to your benefit. Table 4 lists foods that contain particularly high amounts of tryptophan and tyrosine.

FATS

Fats in the body are divided into two types. The first is fats that are stored in the fatty tissues as potential fuel and that, under emergency conditions (especially when the body has an insufficient amount of sugar or under conditions of starvation and hunger), can be broken down and metabolized. The second kind of fats, called phospholipids, are important constituents of the membranes that form the outer border of cells inside the body and that, with proteins, form some of the structures within cells. The amount of phospholipids in the body at any given time is independent of the state of nutrition, whereas the fats used as fuel may weigh less than 10 pounds in a thin individual and as much as 150 pounds in an obese person. People tend to think of fat as harmful because it is involved in certain circumstances in clogging arteries. But fat is also a basic component of cell structure throughout the body and a chemical building block of vital hormones.

When fats are ingested in any quantity, they slow the emptying of the stomach and produce a certain mental sluggishness that has both advantages and disadvantages. A relatively high-fat meal should never be eaten if it is to be followed by a highly challenging or concentrated effort that requires a great deal of attention. In contrast, individuals who have reactive hypoglycemia, which may result from taking excessive sugar (producing an increased amount of insulin secretion) can use a diet with increased polyunsaturated fatty acids to produce a more even flow of glucose and ketone bodies into the bloodstream. This process is facilitated when the glucose ingested is in the form of starch.

Cholesterol, which is also a kind of fat that is present in cell membranes along with saturated fatty acids, plays a role in the clogging of arterial lumens with atherosclerotic plaques. While cholesterol is essential in the production of hormones and bile salts, we don't have to take extra amounts because it is manufactured within the human body.

We hear a lot of people tell us that excess cholesterol is bad for us, but in fact genetics plays a major role in determining for whom it is and is not harmful. Not everyone has to avoid cholesterol, as I learned from an experience in my own family. In the mid-1950s, one of my uncles was diagnosed as having conduction heart problems, and the therapy his doctor prescribed for him then was an all-egg diet that was loaded with cholesterol. My guess is that he was misdiagnosed, but he followed the advice and was never bothered by heart problems again. He lived into his early nineties, so his cholesterol-rich diet certainly did him no harm.

Saturated fats, the kind that act with cholesterol to produce arterial disease, are present in many foods, especially processed food sold in supermarkets or at fast food chains. Many of the foods that taste good, like wieners, ham, and the better cuts of steak, are loaded with saturated fats. Some small amount of fat in one's diet is unavoidable and not particularly troublesome. It becomes a problem only in people who have a history of heart disease or hardening of the arteries.

Since you will be taking in some fats every day, you should know that the best kinds are those in the form of unsaturated fatty acids. The wrong kind of fat, namely the saturated or hard fats, are present in lard, butter, cream, ice cream, and shortening. As a general rule, fats that are liquid at room temperature are apt to be unsaturated and better for you than those that are saturated and in the solid state. (Coconut oil, which contains a saturated fatty acid, is an exception to this rule.)

CARBOHYDRATES, SUGARS, AND STARCHES

I've seen a fair amount of confusion in the faces of my patients when I start telling them about starches, sugars, and carbohydrates. The reason, I think, is that most people don't really understand how they're related. Carbohydrates, which are simple molecules made by plants, include sugars and starches. When starches metabolize they break down into sugars. That's really all you have to know to understand what I'm going to tell you.

Starch is present in cereal products and root vegetables such as potatoes and beans. The products of digested starch are always sugars. When your body needs energy, it metabolizes the sugar molecules with the aid of insulin from the pancreas.

Whether you eat starches or sugars can make a big difference to your mental alertness. Starches are broken down more gradually to effect a slow release of sugar, so your body doesn't have to produce an excess of insulin to metabolize the sugar. However, if large amounts of sugar are introduced into the bloodstream at any one time, an excessive amount of insulin may be generated that will produce a rebound effect and a low blood sugar. You may get feelings of tremulousness and anxiety, which is certainly not the environment for optimal brain function.

FRUITS, VEGETABLES, AND FIBER

There are two varieties of fruits, and their nutritional value for the brain power diet varies widely. Dates or dried figs add a substantial amount of potassium, calcium, and phosphorus to the diet, as well as magnesium, zinc, and iron, but they both contain very little vitamin C. Cantaloupe contains a substantial amount of vitamin A as well as vitamin C and vitamin B_9, while oranges and other citrus fruits contain adequate amounts of vitamin A, vitamin C, and vitamin B$_9$, as well as potassium, calcium, phosphorus, and magnesium.

The point is that dried fruits are a rich source of minerals but are low in vitamin content, while fresh fruits are just the opposite: high in certain vitamins and low in minerals. Both kinds are good to have in your diet for variety, but you should know what the differences are.

The contribution of vegetables to the brain power diet is significant, but again you have to be an astute consumer. Broccoli, spinach, and cauliflower have substantial amounts of vitamin C and minerals, including calcium, magnesium, and iron, but very little vitamin B$_3$ (niacin). Vegetables such as avocados, mushrooms, black-eyed peas, and collard greens do have a substantial amount of vitamin B$_3$, but they have less vitamin C.

If you study the nutrient content of various fruits and vegetables, you'll see that the amounts of nutrients present are insufficient to fulfill the requirements of the brain power diet unless you eat enormous quantities of everything. Except for vitamin C, vitamin A, and potassium, the foods that would be the mainstays of a vegetarian diet will not provide you with anywhere close to an optimal amount of nutrients, vitamins, minerals, and electrolytes. This is why I strongly recommend supplemental vitamins, minerals, nutrients, and electrolytes to people who want to eat fruits and vegetables exclusively.

No matter what your diet consists of, I believe you can benefit from eating cereals and grain products because many of these products contain fiber. Fiber in the form of bran not only supplies some of the B vitamins but because much of it (the insoluble fiber in wheat bran) is not absorbed and because it swells up with the addition of water, it tends to fill the distended stomach and prevent hunger pangs. Wheat bran is great for people on calorie-restricted diets because the body cannot absorb much of the product, so it contributes practically nothing to caloric intake. It also softens the stool, which means that the regular intake of this substance reduces the incidence of cancer of the colon. Oat bran, more of which is absorbed, has the capacity for reducing the serum cholesterol.

BEVERAGES

Most of the body is made up of water, and even normal, functioning kidneys require a certain minimum intake of water each day to clear the blood of waste products. Because an excessive amount of water or a deficiency of water can alter the concentration of electrolytes such as sodium, potassium, and chloride, water has a profound effect on brain function.

Recently, the importance of water to brain function was driven home to me in a very immediate way. Sarah, a sixty-two-year-old woman of Polish descent, came to me with a tangerine-sized tumor on the surface of her brain that turned out to be a meningioma (a benign tumor). I removed the tumor in a routine operation, and I was confident that she would make an uneventful recovery. My predictions were certainly accurate for the first two or three days because she began to talk sensibly, had normal vision, and moved her extremities purposefully. On the third postoperative day she was able to sit up in a chair. However, on day four she didn't look quite so well, and she began to have difficulty staying awake. Sometime during the middle of the night, she complained of a headache, became confused, and then suffered an epileptic seizure.

I first thought that something had gone wrong with the operation. I knew that the tumor had been completely removed, but I was afraid that she had some bleeding in her brain or on the surface of it and would require emergency attention. All of the neurological tests showed that this was not the case, however. There was no evidence of bleeding, although the CAT scan showed that the brain was swollen and her lateral ventricles were very small.

Blood studies pinpointed the problem. Sarah had a temporary disturbance in the blood level of antidiuretic hormone secreted from her posterior pituitary that lasted for two days. As a result she was very thirsty and was drinking a substantial amount of water, in addition to the fluids she was getting intravenously. Whereas the electrolytes in the fluids in her IV bottles were balanced, the water she was drinking had no electrolytes and she quickly became overhydrated, resulting in a depressed level of sodium. Strict fluid restriction allowed her serum sodium to rise to normal levels, and her symptoms disappeared.

In most cases, I have to worry about people taking in too little water rather than too much. Even in people with normal kidney function, one to two liters (thirty to sixty ounces) of water, or water equivalents, a day is recommended. Not all of the water has to be in the form of liquid. Many foods contain a substantial proportion of water, and of course water is present in soups, juices, dairy products, and other beverages.

Many people wonder whether they should be drinking as much coffee as they do, particularly when so much has been written about its capacity to make people "nervous." The controversy about coffee really centers around its caffeine content. Caffeine is a brain stimulant, and a small amount of it is not harmful. However, the brain develops a tolerance for caffeine, so that people who drink a substantial amount of coffee begin to *require* the stimulant just to feel right and function normally. This is also true with tea, but to a lesser extent.

Soft drinks like Coca-Cola, Dr. Pepper, Pepsi, RC Cola, and Shasta also contain significant amounts of caffeine, but their sugar content is more troublesome. Some diet beverages, including Diet Coke, Diet Pepsi, and diet root beer, contain artificial sweeteners such as aspartame. A number of studies on artificial sweeteners have supposedly linked them to alteration in brain function and changes in behavior. Several of the studies were reviewed in a *New England Journal of Medicine* article in 1983, but the results were inconclusive and the findings were disputed by a number of traditional dietitians. Since then, not much of consequence has been added to this debate.

My own nonscientific observations of people who drink more

than a liter of diet beverages a day is that they sometimes become hyperirritable, and they seem to have the same need for diet beverages that other people have for tobacco products. I haven't done a control study on this, and I'm not aware of decisive studies by either the critics or proponents of sweeteners, but I'm a little wary of them.

I've already discussed alcohol in earlier chapters, but I will remind you here that alcohol is a habit-forming substance and a brain poison. Although people who drink regularly develop partial protective mechanisms to detoxify the alcohol, the effect is amelioration rather than elimination of the poisoning effect on the brain. Alcohol is comparable to cocaine, marijuana, speed, barbiturates, and PCPs in terms of its distortion of brain function. This does not mean that all these drugs act in a similar way or all have the same effect; they do not. What I want to emphasize is that they all distort brain function. They reduce, rather than enhance, your brain power and your ability to master your environment.

DAIRY PRODUCTS

Skim milk is an excellent food for individuals who do not have a lactose intolerance. It provides a substantial amount of protein, vitamin A, some of the B vitamins, and a substantial amount of electrolytes and minerals. It is low in vitamin C but has a full complement of amino acids, including tryptophan and tyrosine, and of course plenty of calcium. Skim milk yogurt is also an excellent source of minerals and certain B vitamins.

Milk products contribute enough sodium to the diet so that it is not necessary to either salt your food or eat any canned foods that contain a lot of sodium. (This includes most canned soups, canned meat, and canned fish, unless the cans are specifically labeled low sodium.) One has to be particularly watchful of the sodium in various cheeses, such as cheddar cheese and creamed cottage cheese. I'm not suggesting that indulging in cheese once in a while is bad for you. However, a diet with a high daily intake of cheese may be related to high blood pressure in susceptible people and to headaches in people who are allergic to tyramine.

BODY CYCLES

I've already alluded to the fact that the amount and quality of the food you eat can have an effect on your moods and performance. A knowledge of the various factors involved can be of use if you've been up all night studying, for example, and have to take a test or if you've spent a sleepless night before an important presentation in the morning to sell a product.

A meal of chicken, turkey, or other fowl and a cup of tea or coffee, if you aren't a caffeine abuser, will prepare you for mental combat and stress. But if you're jittery and nervous and haven't been able to sleep, a meal high in starch, such as a bowl of popcorn or a baked potato, will help smooth out the wrinkles of unproductive brain excitation.

For longer cycles, a more consistent dietary strategy is needed. Your diet should be planned for your general well-being and health, not just for emergencies. For a consistent, productive mental effort, special diets should be used only in extraordinary circumstances so that they don't become a habit that leads to declines in your performance.

All biological systems, including human beings, are cyclic. We sleep during the night and are awake during the day. Our temperature and the concentration of various hormones in our bodies varies throughout the day, depending on our daily, or circadian, rhythm. Our needs vary from week to week and season to season. The menstrual cycle or pregnancy imposes a different set of dietary imperatives that influence the intake of nutrients, vitamins, minerals, and electrolytes. These factors are different from person to person.

How then can you determine the best time for you to eat? This question is almost impossible to answer if you are either overweight or underweight. For most of us who are in between, however, nature tells us when we need food. Hunger is a natural phenomenon, and when we're not hungry we don't need to force food on ourselves. We do need to be careful not to nibble away all day long to assuage anxiety. I'd like to assure you that whether you eat only one or two meals a day or have three, five, or seven meals, you will not be harming your body as long as you restrict your caloric intake to the amount that you need and use and as long as you don't use eating as a treatment for anxiety. If you have a tendency toward reactive hypoglycemia or feelings of tremulousness, more frequent meals with smaller quantities of food and calories may help you function more efficiently and help your brain perform more effectively. Experiment with different eating patterns to see which ones work best for you.

TIPS FOR WEIGHT LOSS AND WEIGHT GAIN

If you're gaining weight or if you're on a reducing diet and are not losing weight at an appropriate pace, it means you have to take in fewer calories. It is important to realize that each gram of protein or carbohydrate contains four and a half calories, while each gram of fat contains nine calories. That means that foods like butter, ice cream, marbled steaks, ham, and bacon will cause you to put on weight because they contain twice as many calories as a similar portion of food with less fat.

Another important strategy for losing weight is to change the amount of food you eat at certain intervals. Your largest meal should be breakfast, and your smallest meal should be dinner. The reason is that the body is a heat machine and you have to stoke it up before you work, not when you come home from work and are ready to drop into bed and allow the excess calories to be stored in your fatty tissue.

It's useful in this regard to eat wheat bran to fill up your stomach and keep hunger pangs away. Bran flakes can be mixed with low-fat or nonfat fruit yogurt and refrigerated to form a confection. Snacks between meals can include fruits, fruit juices, vegetables such as carrots and celery, and salads without dressing. You'll be amazed at some of the wholesome flavors contained in vegetables when you taste them without the strong spices and garlic that are so common in most salad dressings. Also keep in mind that if you take in too much salt you will have a tendency to retain fluid so that even with a reduced-calorie intake, water retention will keep your weight at an undesirable level.

ALLERGIES ASSOCIATED WITH SOME BRAIN FOODS

The intake of food is often associated with strong emotions. It is probably not surprising that unfavorable responses to a particular food may be largely emotional rather than allergic. However, some natural foods contain substances such as histamine and tyramine that can produce symptoms. The headaches of one well-known food intolerance syndrome, for example, are directly attributable to tyramine. Many of the amines have a powerful effect on blood vessels, particularly blood vessels in the brain. The amines, which are contained in certain red wines and cheeses, may give rise to severe headaches that are difficult to distinguish from migraines.

The so-called Chinese restaurant syndrome may be related to food additives. A physician reported in 1968 that he suffered from numbness on the back of his neck, which radiated into both arms and was accompanied by weakness and palpitations, while eating at a Chinese restaurant. The syndrome lasted two hours and left no hangover. Detective work found that the syndrome was related to the food additive monosodium glutamate, or MSG. (The Chinese use both seaweeds and soybeans, which contain sodium glutamate, as a flavor for foods.) Artificial MSG is a flavor enhancer widely used in the food industry.

Food intolerance, which in some cases may be related to an allergy, is most often seen in people under thirty years of age, and it is rare after age sixty. In a study done at Guy's Hospital in London, the foods that most often caused intolerance were milk, eggs, peanuts, fish, flour, and chocolate. Symptoms people have had include asthma, nausea and vomiting, eczema, hives, runny nose, and swelling of the lips. Fortunately, the treatment is simple: Avoid the offending food. Occasionally the proteins that cause the problems in specific foods can be denatured by heat, which makes them safe to eat. Hives are often effectively controlled by antihistamines, and severe attacks can be treated by steroids.

Above all, the offending food substance must be identified and eliminated from the diet. Some patients, even some of those who are quite sophisticated, become so emotionally reactive to their supposed food intolerance that they eliminate many foods unnecessarily. As a consequence they may become very undernourished. Accurate testing is essential so that only those foods that cause the symptoms and the food intolerance are eliminated.

Some people, unfortunately, have multiple food intolerances. If you fall into this category, you'll have to find those foods that you do tolerate and supplement your diet with adequate amounts of nutrients, vitamins, minerals, and electrolytes in the form of pills or powder. You must also ensure an adequate intake of calories because some people in this predicament experience an undesirable weight loss. One of the best ways to do this is to substitute fat, in the form of unsaturated fatty acids, for carbohydrates or protein, since one gram of the fatty acids contains twice as many calories as a gram of protein or carbohydrate. This is the opposite process from the one I described for weight loss. Just as with diets for weight loss, diets to promote weight gain have to be nutritionally balanced to ensure that good health is maintained.

Chapter 11

Meals and Menus
for Maximum
Brain Power

GETTING STARTED

On the next few pages, I have outlined a schedule of foods that
contain the essential brain power nutrients I discussed earlier.
This is not a strict, step-by-step program. My purpose in listing
two weeks of sample menus is to suggest ways to incorporate
various low-fat brain power foods into a balanced diet. It is also
to get you accustomed to a change in eating patterns that will be
healthier for you in the long run no matter which foods you eat.

When you look at the menus you should notice not just what's
there but also what's missing. A few of the things you won't find
are butter, whole milk, ice cream, fast foods, and processed foods.
While this is not specifically a weight loss diet, those foods
contain large amounts of hard fat and salt, two items that work
against the maintenance of a healthy body and stable weight, so
I advise you to avoid them.

Also, while there are no recipes in this book, I advise you not
to cook any of the foods listed here with hard, saturated fats or
lard. You can safely assume that if a fried food is listed, it is to

be prepared with corn oil or safflower oil. You may substitute one food for another as long as the substitutes meet the criteria of being low in fat and low in sodium. Whenever a low-salt alternative is available, I recommend that you choose it.

In general, the menus I present in this chapter are designed along these lines: The first meal of the day should start off with fresh fruit or fresh juice followed by a main dish such as chicken, turkey, tuna, or an egg. In addition, have a muffin or bread and coffee or tea. This is a larger meal than most of us have for breakfast, so it may take a while to get used to consuming more calories early in the day.

When you feel hungry, you can have a mid-morning snack of either a fruit, some vegetables, or some whole grain bread or muffin. I don't recommend anything more substantial because you'll have your second meal shortly thereafter.

Your second meal should start with a salad, followed by a main dish of either seafood or poultry. You can also have a very lean red meat dish every third day, so long as the fat and sodium content of the foods is low. With your main dish, have some vegetables, such as potatoes, carrots, or green beans. You may have any kind of dessert so long as it doesn't contain shortening or butter. I recommend fruit-based pies (pie crust made with oil instead of shortening) or fresh berries, but you can also have some sweet muffins or a pudding.

For a mid-afternoon snack, try unsalted nuts of various kinds, yogurts, raisins, dates, or fresh fruit. The object is just to keep your energy level up rather than to fill you up. I caution against the urge to eat a candy bar as a mid-afternoon snack because the high sugar content will give you a temporary "sugar high," which will rapidly be followed by an insulin-inspired "sugar low." This kind of dramatic mood swing is not good for your mental health.

The last meal of the day should be eaten several hours before you go to bed so that you have a chance to digest the food while you are still moderately active. Start with a fruit juice and salad, and then have a small portion of seafood or poultry or a soft-boiled egg, a small quantity of fresh vegetables, a small dinner roll, and a small portion of dessert. You can also have some skim milk or tea, but I do not recommend coffee because it will mentally stimulate you when you should be gearing down.

When you look at the menus for the third meal, you might at first think the meals are large because I've included a lot of different foods. The portions, however, are quite small, and you should carefully observe them. Some families may have to make some adjustments in their eating patterns. In this country, most of us have been brought up to think of the dinner hour, from six to seven, as a time when everyone sits down around the table for a large feast. I think the idea of family dinners is great, but we should have a smaller meal at that time.

Most people have a tendency to overeat during the time of day when they are least active, and such eating habits can lead into a cycle of lethargic evenings and sluggish mornings. If you eat more sparingly in the evening, you'll wake up hungry in the morning (which is how you should feel), and you'll have no trouble eating a full breakfast. Give yourself a few weeks to get used to the change in eating schedule and see if you notice a difference. Keep in mind that it may take your body some time to adjust to this new regimen.

SUPPLEMENTS

The maintenance diet on the next few pages will not, by itself, give you *optimal* doses of all the vitamins and minerals. This is especially true for women who lead sedentary lives because their calorie requirements are so low. You will get all of the fat-soluble vitamins A, D, and E that you need, as well as enough amino acids, minerals, electrolytes, and water. But you won't get enough of the water-soluble B vitamins, choline, or vitamin C.

Most pharmacies and all health food stores carry separate bottles of vitamin B supplement, vitamin C, and choline in various forms, including powders, pills, and liquids. At whatever meal you prefer, take one supplement of each. Make sure that the doses for each vitamin and choline are at least as follows:

Vitamin C	1000 mg
Vitamin B_1	20 mg
Vitamin B_2	10 mg
Vitamin B_3 (niacinamide)	250 mg
Vitamin B_5	20 mg
Vitamin B_6	20 mg
Vitamin B_9	1 mg
Vitamin B_{12}	100 mcg
Choline	3 g

As a convenience, Schiff has distributed a combination of vitamins and minerals to conform to the recommendations in this book, except for choline, which must be taken separately. This supplement can be found in all health food stores.

If you follow my maintenance diet and take the supplements, you'll actually get somewhat more of each vitamin than you need. In these amounts they do not have any toxic or side effects that you need to be worried about, and you'll get adequate amounts of each even if you have to skip a meal.

14-DAY BRAIN POWER
MAINTENANCE DIET FOR MEN*

WEEK 1 / DAY 1

Meal 1
Orange slices
Broiled salmon (3.5 oz.)
Bran muffin (made with corn oil)
Tea/water

Snack
2 slices toasted whole wheat bread
Cottage cheese, low fat (1 cup)

Meal 2
Fruit cup (½ cup)
Tossed salad with low-cal dressing

*Both this diet and the diet for women were analyzed using the CBORD Professional Diet Analyzer. The ingredients assumed in the computer program are not necessarily the same ones advocated in this book. Therefore, if you follow the guidelines suggested here, your actual calorie, fat, and cholesterol intake will be less.

14-DAY BRAIN POWER
MAINTENANCE DIET FOR MEN

Very lean hamburger (3 oz.)
Blueberry muffin (made with corn
  oil)
Coffee/tea

Snack
Fruit-flavored yogurt or skim milk
  (1 cup)

Meal 3
Medallions of fruit (melon and
  grapes) ($\frac{1}{4}$ cup)
Soft-boiled egg
Mashed potatoes ($\frac{1}{2}$ cup) and
  peas ($\frac{2}{3}$ cup)
Dinner roll
Gelatin dessert ($\frac{1}{2}$ cup)
Tea/water

CALORIES: 1650
FAT: 38.2 g
CHOLESTEROL: 472.9 mg

WEEK 1 / DAY 2
Meal 1
Apple juice (8 oz.)
Soy burger or tofu burger with
  relish
Cornbread
Coffee (no cream)

Snack
Crunchy cold raw vegetables
  (carrots, broccoli)
Bran muffin (made with corn oil)

Meal 2
Caesar salad with low-cal dressing
Broiled swordfish or halibut or

trout (3.5 oz.)
Mashed potatoes ($\frac{1}{2}$ cup), peas
  and corn (1 cup)
Applesauce ($\frac{1}{2}$ cup) and biscuit
Tea

Snack
Unsalted cashews ($\frac{1}{10}$ cup)

Meal 3
Orange juice (8 oz.)
Baked stuffed pepper (no meat)
Green beans ($\frac{1}{2}$ cup)
Custard pie (1 small piece)
Tea/water

CALORIES: 1750
FAT: 55.0 g
CHOLESTEROL: 447.4 mg

WEEK 1 / DAY 3
Meal 1
Honeydew melon ($\frac{1}{4}$ cup)
Broiled chicken ($\frac{1}{2}$ breast without
  skin)
Bran muffin (made with corn oil)
Coffee/tea/water

Snack
Cornbread (1 serving)

Meal 2
Sliced fruit
Broiled salmon (3.5 oz.)
Hash brown potatoes ($\frac{1}{2}$ cup)
Deep dish apple pie (1 small piece)
Coffee (no cream)

Snack
Unsalted peanuts (1 oz.)

14-DAY BRAIN POWER
MAINTENANCE DIET FOR MEN

Meal 3
Tomato juice (8 oz.)
Mushroom and onion omelet
Green salad with low-cal dressing
Angel food cake (1 small piece)
Tea/water

CALORIES: 1500
FAT: 58.4 g
CHOLESTEROL: 431.1 mg

WEEK 1 / DAY 4

Meal 1
Applesauce (½ cup)
Albacore tuna steak (4 oz.)
Toasted bran muffin (made with oil)
Coffee/tea/water

Snack
Cold vegetables (carrots, celery, broccoli)

Meal 2
White breast turkey sandwich on rye bread (3 oz.)
Lettuce, tomato, and low-fat mayonnaise
Rhubarb pie (1 piece)
Coffee/tea/low-fat milk

Snack
Low-salt peanut butter on 1 slice whole wheat bread

Meal 3
Grapefruit slices
Broiled chicken breast (½ breast without skin)

Corn (½ cup)
Dinner roll
Sponge cake (1 small piece)
Tea/water

CALORIES: 1800
FAT: 52.9 g
CHOLESTEROL: 470.0 mg

WEEK 1 / DAY 5

Meal 1
Sliced pear (½ cup)
Poached egg on whole wheat toast
Cottage cheese, low fat (1 cup)
Coffee/tea/low-fat milk

Snack
Bran muffin (made with corn oil)
Tea/water

Meal 2
Fresh strawberries (1 cup)
Vegetable salad
Baked stuffed chicken (4 oz.)
Coffee/tea/water

Snack
Banana

Meal 3
Tossed green salad
Haddock with lemon
Mashed potatoes (1 cup), corn (¼ cup), and yellow beans (¼ cup)
Angel food cake (1 small piece)

CALORIES: 1500
FAT: 36.1 g
CHOLESTEROL: 505.0 mg

14-DAY BRAIN POWER
MAINTENANCE DIET FOR MEN

WEEK 1 / DAY 6

Meal 1
Mixed berries (½ cup)
Tuna fish salad (½ cup)
Bran muffin (made with corn oil)
Coffee/tea/water

Snack
Black olives (4 med.)

Meal 2
Tomato juice (8 oz.)
Chicken pot pie (4 oz.)
Mixed green salad
Cornbread
Coffee/tea/water

Snack
Chicken livers (3.5 oz.) on rye
  bread

Meal 3
Citrus fruit assortment
Meat loaf (lean beef) (3.5 oz.)
Baked potato, broccoli and carrots
  (1.5 cups)
Oatmeal cookies (2)
Tea/water

CALORIES: 1600
FAT: 52.9 g
CHOLESTEROL: 643.1 mg

WEEK 1 / DAY 7

Meal 1
Tomato salad
Hard-boiled egg
Blueberry muffin

Coffee/tea/water

Snack
Fruit yogurt
Bran muffin

Meal 2
Tofu or soy burger on toasted bun
  (4 oz.)
Tossed green salad with low-fat
  dressing
Apple pie (1 slice)
Coffee/tea/water

Snack
Cold vegetables (carrots,
  cauliflower)

Meal 3
Cantaloupe (½ cup)
Poached salmon (3.5 oz.)
Broiled potato (½ cup), onions
  and peas (½ cup)
Mixed salad
Butterscotch pudding (⅖ cup)
Tea/water

CALORIES: 1600
FAT: 47.0 g
CHOLESTEROL: 408.1 mg

WEEK 2 / DAY 1

Meal 1
Fresh apple or fresh pear
Turkey sandwich on whole wheat
  bread (3 oz.)
Bran muffin (made with corn oil)
Coffee/tea/water

14-DAY BRAIN POWER MAINTENANCE DIET FOR MEN

Snack
Fruit yogurt (1 cup)

Meal 2
Vegetable soup or consommé
  (1 cup)
Roast chicken breast (½ breast
  without skin)
Tossed salad
Blueberry pie (½ piece)

Snack
Fresh raw carrot sticks

Meal 3
Fresh honeydew melon
Spinach soufflé (4 oz.)
Mixed vegetables (⅔ cup)
Whole wheat muffin (made with
  corn oil)
Lemon-lime sherbet (1 cup)
Tea/water

CALORIES: 1800
FAT: 41.6 g
CHOLESTEROL: 206.2 mg

WEEK 2 / DAY 2
Meal 1
Honeydew melon or cantaloupe
  (½ cup)
Lean roast beef sandwich on whole
  wheat
Blueberry muffin or rye toast
Coffee/tea/water/skim milk

Snack
Fresh carrot sticks

Meal 2
Tomato or V-8 juice (8 oz.)
Steamed scallops (4 med.)
Au gratin potatoes (½ cup)
Peas and carrots (1⅓ cups)
Gelatin dessert (½ cup)

Snack
Sunflower seed kernels (unsalted)
  (1 oz.)

Meal 3
Fruit cocktail (½ cup)
Spaghetti and tomato sauce (no
  meat) (1 cup)
Asparagus (1 cup)
Sponge cake (1 small piece)
Tea/water

CALORIES: 1850
FAT: 51.6 g
CHOLESTEROL: 420.3 mg

WEEK 2 / DAY 3
Meal 1
Fresh strawberries (1 cup)
Cheese-mushroom omelet
Whole wheat toast (1 slice)
Coffee/tea/water/skim milk

Snack
1 orange or apple

Meal 2
Sectioned grapefruit
Broiled salmon (3.5 oz.)
Wild/brown rice (½ cup)
Peas, beans, and broccoli (¾ cup)

14-DAY BRAIN POWER
MAINTENANCE DIET FOR MEN

Danish pastry (1 piece)

Snack
Fruit yogurt (1 cup)

Meal 3
Tossed green salad
Chicken pot pie (4 oz.)
Peas and carrots (½ cup)
Rice pudding (⅔ cup)
Tea/water

CALORIES: 1900
FAT: 63.1 g
CHOLESTEROL: 425.4 mg

WEEK 2 / DAY 4

Meal 1
Fresh grapefruit
Hard-boiled egg or poached egg on
    toast
Raisin-blueberry muffin (made
    with corn oil)
Coffee/tea/water

Snack
1 apple or pear

Meal 2
Tossed salad with apples and
    raisins
Fried shrimp (3.5 oz.)
Chocolate custard (½ cup)

Snack
Chive cottage cheese, low fat
    (1 cup)

Meal 3
Fresh orange juice (8 oz.)

Macaroni and cheese (8 oz.)
Tomato slices
Whole wheat dinner roll
Tea/water

CALORIES: 1700
FAT: 56.5 g
CHOLESTEROL: 690.0 mg

WEEK 2 / DAY 5

Meal 1
Fresh grapefruit juice (8 oz.)
Chicken salad sandwich on whole
    wheat
Coffee/tea/water/skim milk

Snack
Celery with low-calorie cottage
    cheese (1 cup)

Meal 2
Fruit cup (½ cup)
Turkey loaf (3.5 oz.)
Sweet potato or baked potato and
    carrots (½ cup)
Chiffon pie (1 small piece)

Snack
Ryekrisp, sesame crackers (2)

Meal 3
Mixed salad
Broiled cod (3.5 oz.)
Acorn squash (1 cup)
Blueberry muffin (made with corn
    oil)
Sponge cake (1 small piece)
Tea/water

14-DAY BRAIN POWER
MAINTENANCE DIET FOR MEN

CALORIES: 2300
FAT: 70.8 g
CHOLESTEROL: 687.0 mg

WEEK 2 / DAY 6

Meal 1
Sweet cherries or apple juice (½ cup)
Tuna salad sandwich on whole wheat bread
Coffee/tea/water

Snack
Bran muffin (made with corn oil)
Tea

Meal 2
Carrot-raisin salad (½ cup)
Sliced turkey sandwich on whole wheat
Sliced tomato
Grapes (1 cup)

Snack
Roasted unsalted almonds (12 nuts)

Meal 3
Tuna-noodle casserole (3.5 oz.)
Green beans (½ cup)
Cornbread
Vanilla or chocolate custard (½ cup)
Tea/water

CALORIES: 1600

FAT: 60.4 g
CHOLESTEROL: 346.0 mg

WEEK 2 / DAY 7

Meal 1
Tomato juice or pineapple juice (8 oz.)
Creamed chicken (3.5 oz.)
Cranberry muffin (made with corn oil)
Coffee/tea/water/skim milk

Snack
Chicken broth (1 cup)
Raisin toast

Meal 2
Fruit cup (1 cup)
Soy burger or tofu burger
Bread pudding with raisins (¾ cup)

Snack
Banana bread

Meal 3
Spinach salad
Salmon patty (3.5 oz.)
Green beans (½ cup)
Orange-lemon sherbet (1 cup)
Tea/water

CALORIES: 1700
FAT: 52.8 g
CHOLESTEROL: 398.9 mg

14-DAY BRAIN POWER
MAINTENANCE DIET FOR WOMEN

WEEK I / DAY I

Meal 1
Orange slices
Broiled salmon (2 oz.)
Bran muffin (made with corn oil)
Tea/water

Snack
1 slice toasted whole wheat bread
Cottage cheese, low fat (½ cup)

Meal 2
Fruit cup (½ cup)
Tossed salad with low-cal dressing
Blueberry muffin (made with corn oil)
Coffee/tea

Snack
Fruit-flavored yogurt or skim milk (½ cup)

Meal 3
Medallions of fruit (melon and grapes) (½ cup)
Soft-boiled egg
Mashed potatoes (¼ cup) and peas (⅔ cup)
Dinner roll
Gelatin dessert
Tea/water

CALORIES: 1100
FAT: 24.3 g
CHOLESTEROL: 388.8 mg

WEEK I / DAY 2

Meal 1
Apple juice (8 oz.)

Soy burger or tofu burger with relish
Cornbread
Coffee (no cream)

Snack
Crunchy cold raw vegetables (carrots, broccoli)
Bran muffin (made with corn oil)

Meal 2
Caesar salad with low-cal dressing
Broiled swordfish or halibut or trout (2 oz.)
Mashed potatoes (¼ cup), peas and corn (½ cup)
Applesauce (½ cup) and biscuit
Tea

Snack
Unsalted cashews (1/10 cup)

Meal 3
Orange juice (8 oz.)
Baked stuffed pepper (no meat) (2 oz.)
Green beans (½ cup)
Custard pie (½ slice)
Tea/water

CALORIES: 1400
FAT: 46.4 g
CHOLESTEROL: 421.5 mg

WEEK I / DAY 3

Meal 1
Honeydew melon (¼)
Broiled chicken (¼ breast without skin)

14-DAY BRAIN POWER
MAINTENANCE DIET FOR WOMEN

Bran muffin (made with corn oil)
Coffee/tea/water

Snack
Cornbread

Meal 2
Sliced fruit
Broiled salmon (2 oz.)
Hash brown potatoes (¼ cup)
Deep dish apple pie (1 small piece)
Coffee (no cream)

Snack
Unsalted peanuts (½ oz.)

Meal 3
Tomato juice (8 oz.)
Mushroom and onion omelet
   (small)
Green salad with low-cal dressing
Angel food cake (1 small piece)
Tea/water

CALORIES: 1250
FAT: 43.9 g
CHOLESTEROL: 381.2 mg

WEEK 1 / DAY 4
Meal 1
Applesauce (½ cup)
Albacore tuna steak (2 oz.)
Toasted bran muffin (made with
   corn oil)
Coffee/tea/water

Snack
Cold vegetables (carrots, celery,
   broccoli)

Meal 2
White breast turkey sandwich on
   rye bread
Lettuce, tomato, and low-fat
   mayonnaise
Rhubarb pie (1 small piece)
Coffee/tea/low-fat milk

Snack
Low-salt peanut butter on 1 slice
   whole wheat bread

Meal 3
Grapefruit slices
Broiled chicken breast (¼ breast
   without skin)
Corn (½ cup)
Dinner roll
Sponge cake (1 small piece)
Tea/water

CALORIES: 1650
FAT: 50.9 g
CHOLESTEROL: 410.5 mg

WEEK 1 / DAY 5
Meal 1
Sliced pear (½ cup)
Poached egg on whole wheat toast
Cottage cheese, low fat (½ cup)
Coffee/tea/low-fat milk

Snack
Bran muffin (made with corn oil)
Tea/water

Meal 2
Fresh strawberries (1 cup)
Vegetable salad

14-DAY BRAIN POWER
MAINTENANCE DIET FOR WOMEN

Baked stuffed chicken (2 oz.)
Coffee/tea/water

Snack
Banana

Meal 3
Tossed green salad
Haddock with lemon (1 small
  piece)
Mashed potatoes (1 cup), corn and
  yellow beans (½ cup)
Angel food cake (1 small piece)

CALORIES: 1200
FAT: 26.7 g
CHOLESTEROL: 437.4 mg

WEEK 1 / DAY 6

Meal 1
Mixed berries (½ cup)
Tuna fish salad (¼ cup)
Bran muffin (made with corn oil)
Coffee/tea/water

Snack
Black olives (4 med.)

Meal 2
Tomato juice (8 oz.)
Chicken pot pie (2 oz.)
Mixed green salad
Cornbread
Coffee/tea/water

Snack
Chicken livers (2 oz.) on rye bread

Meal 3
Citrus fruit assortment

Meat loaf (lean beef) (2 oz.)
Broccoli and carrots (1.5 cups)
Oatmeal cookies (2)
Tea/water

CALORIES: 1100
FAT: 35.7 g
CHOLESTEROL: 397.3 mg

WEEK 1 / DAY 7

Meal 1
Tomato salad
Hard-boiled egg
Blueberry muffin (made with corn
  oil)
Coffee/tea/water

Snack
Fruit yogurt (½ cup)
Bran muffin (made with corn oil)

Meal 2
Tofu or soy burger on toasted bun
Tossed green salad with low-fat
  dressing
Apple pie (1 slice)
Coffee/tea/water

Snack
Cold vegetables (carrots,
  cauliflower)

Meal 3
Cantaloupe (½ cup)
Poached salmon (2 oz.)
Onions and peas (½ cup)
Mixed salad
Butterscotch pudding (⅖ cup)
Tea/water

14-DAY BRAIN POWER
MAINTENANCE DIET FOR WOMEN

CALORIES: 1300
FAT: 44.3 g
CHOLESTEROL: 386.1 mg

WEEK 2 / DAY 1

Meal 1
Fresh apple or fresh pear
Turkey sandwich on whole wheat
    bread
Bran muffin (made with corn oil)
Coffee/tea/water

Snack
Fruit yogurt (½ cup)

Meal 2
Vegetable soup or consommé
Roast chicken breast (¼ breast
    without skin)
Tossed salad
Blueberry pie (½ piece)

Snack
Fresh raw carrot sticks

Meal 3
Fresh honeydew melon (½ cup)
Spinach soufflé (2 oz.)
Mixed vegetables (⅔ cup)
Whole wheat muffin
Lemon-lime sherbet (½ cup)
Tea/water

CALORIES: 1350
FAT: 33.1 g
CHOLESTEROL: 149.6 mg

WEEK 2 / DAY 2

Meal 1

Honeydew melon or cantaloupe
    (½ cup)
Lean roast beef sandwich on whole
    wheat
Blueberry muffin or rye toast
Coffee/tea/water/skim milk

Snack
Fresh carrot sticks

Meal 2
Tomato or V-8 juice (8 oz.)
Steamed scallops (4 med.)
Peas and carrots (1⅓ cups)
Gelatin dessert (½ cup)

Snack
Sunflower seed kernels (unsalted)
    (½ oz.)

Meal 3
Fruit cocktail (½ cup)
Spaghetti and tomato sauce (no
    meat) (2 oz.)
Asparagus (1 cup)
Sponge cake (1 small piece)
Tea/water

CALORIES: 1450
FAT: 34.3 g
CHOLESTEROL: 401.6 mg

WEEK 2 / DAY 3

Meal 1
Fresh strawberries (1 cup)
Cheese-mushroom omelet (small)
Whole wheat toast (1 slice)
Coffee/tea/water/skim milk

14-DAY BRAIN POWER
MAINTENANCE DIET FOR WOMEN

Snack
1 orange or apple

Meal 2
Sectioned grapefruit
Broiled salmon (2 oz.)
Wild/brown rice (¼ cup)
Peas, beans, and broccoli (¾ cup)
Cinnamon streusel (1 piece)

Snack
Fruit yogurt (1 cup)

Meal 3
Tossed green salad
Chicken pot pie (2 oz.)
Peas and carrots (½ cup)
Indian pudding (½ cup)
Tea/water

CALORIES: 1600
FAT: 50.4 g
CHOLESTEROL: 382.6 mg

WEEK 2 / DAY 4

Meal 1
Fresh grapefruit
Hard-boiled egg or poached egg on
  toast
Raisin-blueberry muffin (made
  with corn oil)
Coffee/tea/water

Snack
1 apple or pear

Meal 2
Tossed salad with apples and
  raisins

Fried shrimp (2 oz.)
Chocolate custard (½ cup)

Snack
Chive cottage cheese, low fat
  (½ cup)

Meal 3
Fresh orange juice (8 oz.)
Macaroni and cheese (4 oz.)
Tomato slices
Whole wheat dinner roll
Tea/water

CALORIES: 1400
FAT: 40.2 g
CHOLESTEROL: 577.7 mg

WEEK 2 / DAY 5

Meal 1
Fresh grapefruit juice (8 oz.)
Chicken salad sandwich on whole
  wheat
Coffee/tea/water/skim milk

Snack
Celery sticks

Meal 2
Fruit cup (½ cup)
Turkey loaf (2 oz.)
Carrots (½ cup)
Chiffon pie (1 small piece)

Snack
Ryekrisp, sesame crackers (2)

Meal 3
Mixed salad

14-DAY BRAIN POWER
MAINTENANCE DIET FOR WOMEN

Broiled cod (2 oz.)
Acorn squash (½ cup)
Blueberry muffin (made with corn
  oil)
Strawberry shortcake (1 small
  piece)
Tea/water

CALORIES: 1700
FAT: 56.6 g
CHOLESTEROL: 585.8 mg

WEEK 2 / DAY 6

Meal 1
Sweet cherries or apple juice
  (½ cup)
Tuna salad sandwich on whole
  wheat bread
Coffee/tea/water

Snack
Bran muffin (made with corn oil)
Tea

Meal 2
Carrot-raisin salad (½ cup)
Sliced turkey sandwich on whole
  wheat bread
Sliced tomato
Grapes (1 cup)

Snack
Roasted unsalted almonds (6 nuts)

Meal 3
Tuna-noodle casserole (2 oz.)
Green beans (½ cup)
Cornbread

Vanilla or chocolate custard
  (½ cup)
Tea/water

CALORIES: 1400
FAT: 45.4 g
CHOLESTEROL: 346.0 mg

WEEK 2 / DAY 7

Meal 1
Tomato juice or pineapple juice
  (8 oz.)
Creamed chicken (2 oz.)
Cranberry muffin (made with corn
  oil)
Coffee/tea/water/skim milk

Snack
Chicken broth (1 cup)
Raisin toast

Meal 2
Fruit cup (½ cup)
Soy burger or tofu burger
Bread pudding with raisins
  (½ cup)

Snack
Banana bread

Meal 3
Spinach salad
Salmon patty (2 oz.)
Green beans (½ cup)
Orange-lemon sherbet (½ cup)
Tea/water

CALORIES: 1200
FAT: 37.9 g
CHOLESTEROL: 323.0 mg

Chapter 12

The Brain Power Exercise Program

B rain function is a dynamic process that is modified continuously through the interaction of your brain with your environment. The sensations of vision, hearing, touch, smell, and taste combine to produce integrated and sophisticated images that shape the way your brain responds and functions. It all takes place through a complex process made possible by the remarkable plasticity of the structure and function of the brain. The plasticity has definite limits, a fact we clearly understand when we see someone who has suffered a brain disease or injury.

By studying how the brain recovers from such insults, we have learned a number of lessons about *increasing* brain power that have been combined into a new science called cognitive rehabilitation therapy or neuropsychological rehabilitation.* The underpinnings of this science come from neurology, and some of the techniques used by its practitioners are founded on well-

---

*An extensive review and description of this field was recently edited by M. J. Meier, A. Benton, and L. Diller. See the Bibliography for more details.

established principles in neuropsychology and rehabilitation medicine. What the science shows me is that it's possible to *improve* mental functioning in normal individuals (non-brain-injured) by using the same techniques that were developed to help brain-injured people recover lost abilities.

Before we get into the area of improving mental abilities, I want to summarize a few concepts about the loss of mental abilities. People with more brain cells withstand injury better than people with fewer; this phenomenon explains why brain injury is tolerated better in children than in adults, who lose brain cells with every year of advancing age. Also, injuries that affect the inner part of the brain and produce memory deficits are more difficult to recover from than injuries to the outer part of the brain. The higher the level of brain function that is compromised, the more prolonged is the recovery time.

It may surprise you that the extent of neuropsychological recovery from brain injury and stroke is related to the individual's educational and intellectual level. The reason, it has been suggested, is that overlearned and practiced functions, such as reading and writing, are more widely represented in the brain and therefore those functions are subject to less immediate impairment after an injury. Similarly, before the discovery of L-dopa (a medical therapy for Parkinson's disease), I and a number of other neurosurgeons performed an operation in the internal part of the brain to cut down on abnormal movements and rigidity in Parkinson patients. The criteria for selecting patients who would benefit from this operation were related to their functional capacity. If, prior to the disease, they were functioning at a superior level, we would most often get a good result from brain surgery. The same operation performed on a person with borderline mental capacity was often unsuccessful, with the potential for brain deficits that did not occur in the person with superior intellectual function.

Handedness, also called cerebral dominance, is another important factor in determining the ultimate course of a brain injury or stroke. Most right-handed individuals have their speech function localized in their left cerebral hemisphere, whereas many left-handed individuals have their speech function distributed between their two hemispheres. After a stroke or brain injury, the left-handed individuals (or those persons who are fortunate enough to be ambidextrous) may have some speech loss, but their recovery is more rapid and complete than patients who are exclusively right-handed.

Although word processing functions in right-handed individuals are limited to the left hemisphere, some associated language skills are present in the right hemisphere, even in right-handed people. These skills are associated with the music and poetry of speech, a function called prosody. Not surprisingly, right-handers who have had a stroke in their left-brain speech centers show a remarkable increase in the metabolic activity of their right hemisphere during their recovery period. Had they developed the use of their right hemisphere before a disease or injury incapacitated their left hemisphere, they would have been much better off.

If our brain function is disturbed, especially by disease or injury, then our ability to control our environment is decreased or even lost. That's why my brain power exercise program is so important. My goal is to help you reach your maximum brain power potential and to help you protect it by teaching you techniques that will preserve your brain power even if you suffer a brain injury or disease. Some brain injuries are so extensive that no amount of training will overcome them, but such injuries are often accompanied by the rapid loss of life. Many common brain injuries and diseases allow for some measure of functional recovery. The strategies for recovery, when applied to the normal brain, will help you achieve and maintain increased brain power.

ATTENTION

One of the most fundamental contributors to brain power is our state of attention, which can be divided into three components:

our state of alertness, which means our mental state of arousal and preparedness to respond to our environment; our ability to select from all the environmental stimuli coming into our brain the specific information that we are going to use for mental processing; and our ability to maintain a sustained concentration or vigilance.

Attention and concentration are important components of all new learning and memory, and the control of attention and vigilance is central to many aspects of brain function. A lack of concentration, a short attention span, and distraction all reduce brain power. The ability to avoid distraction and augment concentration skills can be developed and cultivated like any learned behavior. By practicing the exercises in this book, you will learn to increase both your attention and concentration skills.

Appendix 2 contains a number of exercises for you to do. They fall into four categories. I briefly explain them here, but consult the appendix to perform the complete exercises. The exercises require the use of a stopwatch and two people, a subject and an examiner. A typical two-person exercise program would go as follows.

In the first set, the subject is instructed to start the watch and stop it at random intervals specified by the examiner, such as 17 seconds, 23 seconds, and 90 seconds. The subject must be vigilant and keep accurate track of the time.

In the second set, the examiner shows the subject various letters of the alphabet written on slips of paper (up to ten) and randomly associates with each letter a certain time interval. For example, *A* may be equal to 2 minutes, *C* to 20 seconds, and so forth. The subject is given time to memorize the letters and their time values before the exercise starts. Then the examiner holds up a letter and instructs the subject to stop the watch when the elapsed time equals the time value of the letter.

For the third exercise set, the subject is asked to start the watch and, without looking at it, stop it when he or she thinks

10 seconds, 15 seconds, 20 seconds (or whatever the examiner requests) has elapsed. The subject practices the exercise until he or she can accurately stop the watch at intervals up to one minute without looking.

The fourth exercise set was developed for the Dutch air force to increase and test the attention and concentration spans of its pilots. In 1955, I used these exercises to test U.S. air force personnel in a simulated high-altitude pressure chamber, but the exercises work just as well at normal atmospheric pressure. Within a strict time limit, such as 10 seconds, the subject is asked to circle every 3 and every *n* in a block of random letters and numbers such as the following.

1 7 5 c   g 1 f g p 4 8 d n r s t f 1 6 5 3 2 8

t 6 4 2   4 d 4 d c t d g h c d d g a c e s d v

d e v f   g 5 6 7 2 4 3 4 6 6 u c g u 7 8 9 o f

v b b m s z x 2 o d e y f s g l f f n f r e g

e t j k s w e r t y i b x s 5 6 7 g 6 s w 2 4

6 8 f y k l   s x 3 s 1 s d c d f e f f g h j k

MEMORY

Whenever someone tells me, "I have a terrible memory. I wish there was something I could do about it," I explain that there are lots of ways to improve one's memory, and rattle off half a dozen exercises the person can learn. "But that's hard work," the person says. "Isn't there some pill I can take to improve my memory?" "Yes," I say, "there are supplements that will help your memory. Just taking supplements alone will help you. If you take the supplements *and* do memory exercises, you'll see even more improvement."

The process of memory has three main components. The first focuses on attention and concentration, a process that we've just discussed. The second is a process called encoding, which is the way the brain converts a perception into an engram — a physical memory representation in the brain. Once engrams are formed in the brain, they are stored there in a so-called memory bank. The third process is known as retrieval, which is the ability to get at the stored memories at an appropriate time or when called for by a new environmental stimulus or our own desire.

Although memory exercises have not been very effective in rehabilitating brain-injured people with memory difficulties, they are very effective in expanding the memory of normal individuals. Once learned, they enhance our ability to retain certain memory techniques following mild brain injuries. Hence, everyone can potentially profit from their use.

A number of researchers have discovered from experimental investigations that a person's memory can be increased manyfold when items to be remembered are associated with images or other known information. These associations are called mnemonics. One image method for enhancing memory is known as the peg system, in which you number and memorize a set of objects ("pegs") that you can later attach to any list of items you want to remember. To create the pegs, you might associate the number 1 with an ice box, the number 2 with a lamp, the number 3 with an adding machine, and so on. Now you can remember any list of items by attaching a peg to each item on the list. For example, if you want to remember to buy milk, bread, and eggs at the store, you can associate milk with an ice box, bread with a lamp, and eggs with an adding machine.

Another memory technique is called acronym building.* An acronym is a word that is formed from the first letters of a series of words, such as ASAP for "as soon as possible" or ZIP (as in

*Acronym building and other mnemonic techniques are described in detail in *The Executive Memory Guide* by H. Hilton (see the Bibliography).

zip code) for "zone improvement plan." Acronyms are handy ways to remember lists of items.

Sometimes when the initial letters don't form an easily recognizable acronym, the letters can become the first letters of words that say something specific or are part of a verse or a catchy phrase. For example, the four types of schizophrenia are simple, catatonic, paranoid, and hebophrenic. They can be remembered by the phrase "*Sick Campers Pack Heavily.*"

Numbers can also be remembered by associations. For example, 5 and 10, nickel and dime; 7 and 11, luck and heaven; sweet 16; 20–20 vision; 52 weeks in a year; 88 keys on a piano; and 365 days in a year all have strong associations that can help you remember a number.

Another overlooked fact about memory is that it is always easier to remember something if it's part of a song or a verse. There is, in fact, a very good anatomical reason for this. Versification and melody are generated chiefly in the nondominant or right hemisphere. When words (which originate in the left hemisphere in most right-handed people) are put together with verse or song, the whole brain and its memory power are focused for optimal retrieval and use. That's why so many people remember the first line or the title line of a song even when the words are almost meaningless or irrelevant. You can make this process work for you by setting something you want to remember to a piece of music you know or like.

These memory techniques do work, sometimes in spectacular fashion. But they have to be used again and again to form ingrained patterns in the brain. Even a Babe Ruth can strike out and an Arnold Palmer can miss a three-foot putt like any ordinary duffer: If you want to succeed, you have to keep practicing. If your preference is for learning poetry or prayers, memorizing them will be just as good an activity for your brain as the material presented in Appendix 2. Experiment with different methods to find what works best for you. Once you discover a method that suits you, incorporate it into a short, daily routine of physical, mental, and relaxation exercises.

MATHEMATICAL ABILITIES

Just as the motor car allowed people to become more sedentary and more susceptible to heart disease, the computer and electronic calculator have allowed the mathematical centers in many of our brains to atrophy. Not only are repeated arithmetic exercises useful as paradigms of concentration and attention, but they also give a symbolism and appreciation of numbers and numerical values that tend to atrophy if they are not used. Furthermore, arithmetic exercises form the most practical core of knowledge for applications that we encounter in daily life.

You can practice doing mathematical computations, such as addition and subtraction, by writing out a few problems on a piece of paper, but better yet is to balance your checkbook each month without the use of a calculator. You can always check yourself with a calculator if you want to make sure there are no mistakes, but just doing the calculations is good mathematical therapy for the brain. I guarantee that it will help you think with more agility in numerical terms. If you want something a little more challenging, I've included a few math exercises in Appendix 2.

DRAWING

Drawing complex figures not only exercises the right hemisphere but is also an important step in the ambidextrous learning process. Making geometrical figures, such as the house included in the mental status exam, will improve your ability to perceive complex visual images, and it is also an excellent way to begin transferring function from one hemisphere to the other when you practice with both hands.

As an exercise, reproduce several complex line drawings with your right hand (even if you are left-handed) while timing yourself with a stopwatch. Next draw the same pictures with your left hand, also timing yourself. After drawing the figures with both hands, try to reproduce one or two of them from memory. Keep a copy of all the drawings, noting the time it took you to complete each one, and watch your improvement after a few trials. The more you practice, the better you'll get, and the better long-term results you'll have. I especially recommend doing this instead of doodling while on the phone. Just make it a part of your everyday life.

LANGUAGE ABILITIES

The more words you know and recognize in English and other languages and the more words you can use intelligently, the greater will be your brain capacity. And all other things being equal, the more resistant your brain will be to injury and disease. Ambidextrous people and most individuals who are left-handed already have a dispersion of their language functions in both hemispheres, which makes them more resistant to disabling injuries and diseases. But even a left-brained, dominantly right-handed individual who suffers a stroke with language disruptions will show increased metabolic activity in the right or nondominant hemisphere during the period of language recovery. This means that training the right hemisphere before injury or disease strikes the left hemisphere will help speech recovery.

If you don't have time to learn and use a second language, you should at least try to increase your vocabulary in English. One method is simply to memorize lists of words and their meanings, but even if this were effective (it usually is not), it certainly is an unpleasant way to spend your time. A more efficient and satisfying technique is to read intelligently written treatises, plays, epic poetry, historical and archeological monographs, essays, and, last but not least, novels. Many of these materials are now available on tape, and you can easily listen to them while driving, cooking, or doing chores. Whether you read books or listen to them on tape, you'll find that the experience will positively influence your long-term language abilities.

The use of words in context and our overall understanding is more important for intelligence than is the memorization of lists of words and meanings from the dictionary. As you read, the printed page should paint a picture in your mind as dynamic, forceful, and interesting as any video display or giant movie screen. This kind of reading facility can be achieved only with a great deal of practice — at minimum, reading one book a month; more reasonably, one book a week; and for people who are motivated and who have the time, one book a day.

A number of other techniques can help you increase and diversify brain participation in generating and understanding language. One method is to associate words with music, a technique that has been used to restructure language in stroke patients who have lost some of their speaking abilities. Another technique is to learn American sign language with the left hand alone if you are exclusively right-handed and with the right hand if you are dominant left-handed.

The exercises I've described are most effective if they are done starting at an early age, and they become less effective with advancing age. Nevertheless, they will allow you to retain communication skills at a much greater level than would someone who must be taught to write with the left hand after a stroke has paralyzed his or her right side. Indeed, any exercises that impart some language abilities to the left hand in a right-handed person will afford increased potential for written expression even if the person suffers a stroke in the dominant hemisphere.

A special word to dominant right-handed individuals. When you start learning to write with your left hand, you'll appreciate the trauma that left-handed people went through when they were forced at an early age to write with their right hand. Everything will seem backward. Here are a few tips. First, don't try to master cursive writing with your left hand, especially if you're over age forty-five. Be satisfied with printing. If you pick up cursive writing easily with your left hand, then you're not truly right-hand dominant but have always been partially ambidextrous. Second, don't put too much pressure on the pen or pencil. The harder you try, the worse your letters will look. Write with a light touch. Finally, try to make all the parts of your letters with a single stroke, even if it means retracing some of the lines you've already made. Appendix 2 includes a few simple exercises you can use to improve this mental faculty. However, learning to use your left hand to write with regularly in your everyday life can be just as effective as practicing the exercises.

READING ALOUD

Many of us have fallen into sloppy speaking habits because we're in a hurry and we don't pronounce words properly. People around us are sometimes less careful than we are and, like it or not, their bad habits influence our speech.

You can change that by taking a couple of minutes a day to read aloud. If you have small children or grandchildren, I encourage you to read books and stories to them. It helps both you and them in ways that go well beyond verbal communication.

If you don't have someone you can read to, try talking into a tape recorder and playing the tape back to recognize words you're not pronouncing properly. Just pick up a newspaper or magazine, or take any passage at random from Shakespeare, Dickens, the Bible, or some other great work of literature. You'll get more out of reading when you speak the words aloud, and you'll reinforce the speaking abilities you have stored in your brain.

BRAIN REST

So far I've described a number of exercises that increase alertness, concentration and attention, memory and arithmetic abilities, drawing abilties, and the dissemination of language skills in the brain. For the brain to work efficiently, these exercises must be punctuated with periods of brain rest. I want to emphasize that brain rest is different from relaxation, such as looking at television or taking a nap. Brain rest means temporarily shutting down some brain functions.

You initiate brain rest in much the same way as you initiate exercises for attention or memory. It doesn't mean just unharnessing the brain and letting it wander like an undisciplined dog that goes wherever its fancy takes it. Getting the brain into a resting state requires discipline and concentration. There are many paradigms for this method, including autohypnosis, which was refined by the psychologist Andrew Salter; the relaxation response, which was described by Herbert Benson; Zen Buddhism; Transcendental Meditation, and many others.

One of the most rapid methods of achieving brain rest is to use the physiological fact that certain portions of the anatomy — the lips, tongue, thumbs, index fingers, and great toes — have more representation on the surface of the brain than other anatomical structures. Thus, if you seat yourself in a comfortable chair without distractions, you can begin to concentrate and focus your attention on relaxing your right thumb, beginning at the tip and working backward to the first joint and then to the second. When you have spent one or two minutes with your eyes closed concentrating on this anatomical structure, you can go on to the index finger of your right hand and repeat the exercise. Next relax the middle finger, the ring finger, and then the little finger. Repeat the procedure with the left hand, beginning again with the thumb.

When you've completed relaxing your left hand, you can focus your relaxation efforts on your tongue, beginning at the tip and working backward. When the tongue is completely relaxed, you can relax the muscles around your lips, beginning first on the right side and then on the left and starting with the upper lip and then the lower lip. Then proceed to the eyelids on the right, beginning first with the upper, then the lower, and transfer to the left side. If you are not totally relaxed, you can proceed to the toes on your feet, beginning with the great toe on your right side.

Biofeedback treatment makes use of these kinds of brain exercises to relieve people of tension headaches. In biofeedback, an electrode is placed on the tense muscle and is connected to a cathode ray oscilloscope. The tenser the muscle, the more frequent the electrical discharges and the higher the amplitude of the electrical response. The electrode can also be hooked up to an audio amplifier so that the subject can hear the contraction of the muscle as a high-pitched tone. If you use the focused relaxation technique while you are connected to the biofeedback mechanism, you will both see and hear the muscles relaxing. The relaxation response has to be learned and practiced, but it can complement the other mental agility exercises that I have described.

A word of caution: Don't start to learn these relaxation exercises when you are tense or upset because under those circumstances they won't work. You should practice them first when you are relaxed so that you develop strong conditioned reflexes that are unaffected by stress.

PHYSICAL EXERCISES

I include physical exercises in this chapter because it is my strong feeling that a minimum of twenty minutes of exercise a day three or four times a week is an absolutely essential requirement for anyone who seriously wants to improve his or her brain power. To some, this will mean getting out of bed with great difficulty and taking a few painful steps with the help of a walker or doing resistance exercises while lying down. Others may be able to do strenuous weightlifting or play an invigorating game of racquet-ball or tennis. Whatever activity you can do or like to do, it's imperative that you make time to do it.

At one time early in my medical career, I devoted many long hours to working and treating the sick in the hospital. Shifts of forty-eight straight hours were not uncommon, and my entire day often consisted of walking from the wards to the operating room and to the emergency room. I consumed meals in as short a time as I could manage because I never knew if I would be called away suddenly and miss eating the rest of my food. After about six years of this routine, I was overweight and in terrible shape.

Fortunately, when I joined the air force in 1955 and was sent overseas, the apartment where I lived in Wiesbaden was on the top floor of a six-floor building — with no elevator. At first, a small task such as taking the groceries up from the first floor seemed like an unbearable chore. It was hard enough to get myself upstairs, let alone carrying ten or twenty pounds of food as well.

It wasn't long before my forced exercise program, and a low-saturated-fat diet that my wife put me on, began to yield unexpected benefits. When I noticed my trousers sagging around my reduced midsection, I started to look forward to climbing those six flights of stairs. In fact, the weight loss and exercise program I achieved just by going home every evening improved my attitude and gave me extra energy.

These days I still keep in shape by jogging for twelve minutes every morning, doing a series of light calisthenics and walking for forty-five minutes at night. Having seen what a burden — both mentally and physically — it is to carry around added weight, I appreciate that real fitness comes only when both the brain and the body are exercised regularly. We often don't fully appreciate the joy of being able to walk or run or exercise until those abilities are taken away from us. Let us choose to use our bodies and minds to their full potential and in so doing begin to truly get the most out of our lives.

Part IV

Brain Power in the 1990s and Beyond

Chapter 13

Looking Ahead

WHAT YOU CAN TEACH YOUR CHILDREN ABOUT BRAIN POWER

If you really want your children to have optimal brain power throughout life, you should begin teaching them the techniques described in this book before the age of six. Ambidextrous writing skills, for example, which enhance integration of verbal information in both hemispheres, should begin in a reasonable fashion in kindergarten or first grade. I use the word "reasonable" because experience teaches us that *forcing* left-handed individuals to write with their right hands can be detrimental.

Forced writing programs in the first half of this century did produce more bilateral brain representation of language in left-handed individuals than might otherwise have occurred. But the single-minded pursuit of changing left-handed writers into right-handed scribblers resulted in some problems of dyslexia and emotional disturbance. Therefore, I do not suggest that right-handed children should be forced to write exclusively with their left hand any more than I suggest the opposite.

I can assure you that writing exercises done on a blackboard, where the size of the letters can be magnified, will have none of the unhappy effects produced by attempts at cursive writing with a pencil or pen on a small piece of paper.

A second suggestion to enhance ambidextrous skills is to teach freehand drawing and the copying of plain line or geometric figures with both hands. As part of this program, the subject of geography should be reinstituted in the elementary school curriculum. It has been shown that children who don't learn geography grow into adults with a diminished capacity for spatial orientation in the larger sense.

Education that focuses on the significance of mathematics also ought to be started at an early age. Specifically, this means that the relationships between multiplication and addition, division and subtraction, the rules of ten, and the ability to do simple arithmetic without paper and pencil should be emphasized in the early grades of elementary school. It is my impression, after having tested many hundreds of people over the last forty years, that the ability to perform mathematical problems without paper and pencil is gradually being lost, a situation that must be corrected.

English, or at least a form of it, is the first language in the United States, and I'm all in favor of that. However, our primary use of English is no excuse to avoid the study of other languages. It is possible for children age three, four, or five years to become fluent and have a small but usable vocabulary in at least four languages. For many reasons, I strongly urge parents to begin foreign language training in at least one other language besides English for their children no later than age three.

We must also teach children to focus their brain power or to concentrate on command. Because of bad habits, some children are able to concentrate only in special or emergency situations. How often do we find that Johnny or Mary brings home a bad report card on which the teacher has written "Poor concentration"?

It seems like such an obvious point, but it has been overlooked by educators for years. While schools give courses in the basics of reading and writing, they fail to teach children how to focus their attention. Concentration can be learned like any other skill, such as playing the piano or speaking French. Indeed, the brain power exercises in Chapter 12 include a series of exercises for concentrating and focusing attention. These exercises, which often use symbols, are not just for adults. They can and should be used as concentration exercises beginning in kindergarten and continuing throughout a child's educational program.

Exercises involving the focus of attention should also include programs for mental relaxation. Autohypnosis (or autosuggestion) or relaxation exercises that incorporate concentration as a primary relaxation mechanism could begin by age six. With practice, these exercises would relieve much of the stress children experience during their school years.

None of the educational programs I recommend here need be regimented. In fact, to do so might defeat their purpose. Learning ought to be fun and rewarding for children. The application of these exercises would go a long way toward meeting those objectives and would produce lifelong benefits for those who acquire the skills.

Beyond these exercises, children should be taught from the time they are able to understand words that the most important organ in their body is their brain and that their ability to enjoy life, control their own destiny, and function as a human being is dependent on retained brain function. They should also be told from the earliest moment of comprehension that they must protect themselves from brain poisons. They need to know that habit-forming stimulants, including tobacco, alcohol, and all kinds of drugs, should be carefully avoided. They must be told to protect their brain from physical injury and to realize that repeated brain injuries are cumulative. Helmets should be worn in all contact sports and while riding bicycles and skateboarding.

The most frequent cause of brain injury, however, is automobile accidents. The best way to reduce the incidence of brain damage from this cause is to insist that all cars be equipped with air bags or at least shoulder harnesses that are automatic and work properly.

Finally, children should have good examples to follow. More important than words to them are actions and the examples that actions portray. Parents and teachers, for example, can't simply say no to drugs or alcohol; they must also be exemplary role models.

A NATIONAL PLAN FOR THE CARE
OF THE ELDERLY

I think that every freshman high school student in the United States ought to have a chance to visit the patients in a nursing home, just to emphasize to students how important it is to conserve their brain tissues from injury or poisoning. Being incarcerated in a long-term care facility is an unpleasant prospect, but one that millions of us will face if something isn't done to correct the present inexorable increase in the number of nursing home candidates. And with more and more Americans living to old age, projections for increasing the number of nursing home beds beyond the present level of 1.5 million show that huge amounts of the federal budget will have to go toward long-term nursing care. What are the alternatives?

First and foremost is a program for preserving brain function and preventing those diseases and injuries that tend to send people, particularly elderly people, into nursing homes. Many of the most useful techniques are outlined in this book. Second is the use of alternative living arrangements, such as conglomerate housing, instead of nursing homes. These facilities often have apartment-like complexes, many with kitchen facilities or restaurants on the premises. Part of the facilities are devoted to the care of people who are unable to live independently, so that if someone becomes ill, he or she can be cared for in a nursing area on the same grounds as the apartment building. Thus, if a couple lived in an apartment and the husband had a stroke, he could be cared for in one of the nursing home beds while his wife continued to live in their apartment in the same compound and could visit her husband regularly.

That kind of arrangement is expensive. Sometimes the apartment facilities are bought and sometimes they are rented, but if the resident of a conglomerate condominium decided that the environment was not suitable and wanted to move out, he or she would lose a good bit of the initial investment.

Another alternative is placing the elderly individual or couple in an extended family setting. This arrangement could be subsidized in a liberal fashion by both the federal and state governments. The cost of care in a nursing home or other long-term care facility is so great that it would actually be a saving to supply the host family (usually the children of the elderly couple) with either tax credits or a cash subsidy. That way they could put an addition on their home or purchase an additional condominium in the same complex so that the parents could live with their children and grandchildren in the same physical setting. In addition, the savings could be used to supplement the grandparents' social security income. Especially in households in which both husband and wife or a single parent is employed during the day, resulting in so-called latchkey children, the presence of grandparents living on the premises would allow an important educational, social, and cultural tie to be formed between generations on an ongoing basis.

I recognize that all of these proposals seem rather utopian, but I also think they are goals that we should work toward. We've got a long way to go before we can initiate these programs on a wide scale because a number of problems need to be worked out. For example, how will it be possible to redevelop the extended family when there is such chaos and dissolution in the nuclear family? Also, many people might be unwilling to make the personal sacrifice that would elevate the family once again as a primary focus of our national existence.

I submit that the alternatives are not very good. The drab sort of social order that is present in the Scandinavian countries, such as Sweden, involves an institutional-like existence for many of the elderly in which they live quite separately from their children. From the point of view of preserving brain function, I believe that elderly people fare better when they are in a mixed environment that includes a number of young, close associates. Nothing is so depressing as life in a colony for the elderly that has little in the way of demands and only dwindling hopes for the future. In places like these, people who may not be incapacitated themselves begin to imitate the actions and behaviors of those people who are substantially brain-impaired.

We have a choice in this country of which model to follow: the one that began in countries with cradle-to-grave social planning like Sweden and is being emulated by some of the colonies for the elderly in Florida, Arizona, and California, or the American family model with the extended family, including the preservation of traditions, socialization, and cultural education between generations. The latter is the only model, with its challenges and responsibilities, that can keep the elderly feeling and acting young.

NEW BEGINNINGS

What have we learned from our study of brain power that will really help people lead richer and more meaningful lives? We know that different optimal levels of nutrients must be provided to pregnant women, nursing mothers, infants, children, and people of all ages. And we know that brain exercises are not sufficient by themselves in situations in which brain capacity is reduced because of less than optimal brain nutrition. Beyond these kinds of basic facts about nutrition and the brain are issues of larger scope dealing with our expectations from and faith in medical science.

More than enough evidence now casts doubt on the traditional theories of nutrition that state that only enough vitamins, minerals, and other nutrients necessary to avoid certain disease states, like pellagra, beriberi or Korsakoff's psychosis, should be taken. For decades, however, we were either misinformed or, at best, inadequately informed about optimal levels.

I believe there have not been enough investigations into the effects of individual vitamins, minerals, or electrolytes on performance or into the combined effects of high-dosage nutrients on brain function as compared to the minimum required levels that prevent clinical disease. New studies should be done with results that will refine dosage levels.

In the meantime, vitamin, mineral, and nutrient supplements should be given to all schoolchildren, especially those from poorer backgrounds in which adequate nutrition may be lacking. If we err, let us err on the side of overnourishment rather than undernourishment.

Besides nutritional studies, we as a country should set other priorities as goals for future research. The budgets of the National Institute of Mental Health, the National Institution of Neurological Diseases and Stroke, and the National Institute of Aging contain sufficient funds that a substantial amount could be spent on methods of preserving brain integrity and brain function.

For example, one of the most common causes of progressive dementia is multi-infarct dementia. (This is often caused by the breaking off of little clots from the lining of the heart or the major blood vessels going to the brain, producing a loss of brain tissue and a progressive loss of intellectual function.) Many thousands of otherwise normal elderly people lose significant amounts of brain function every year and become helpless and unable to take care of themselves because of this disease.

There is no reason why we should not develop methods for early detection and effective prevention to stop this process before it produces irreversible brain damage. Some of the procedures that have been used to minimize coronary thrombosis or to prevent emboli coming from the major veins in the leg or pelvis from reaching the lung may be modified to prevent emboli from occluding small blood vessels in the brain. New diagnostic techniques using radioactive tracers might detect the onset of these emboli before they break off in the brain's blood vessels, and, most important, new preventive measures using medicines that dissolve clots or keep them from forming might well be applied to a larger percentage of the elderly population.

The same dietary regimens that are used to keep atheromatous plaques from forming in the blood vessels of the heart might also be effective in reducing the number of such plaques in blood vessels going to the brain. Control of serum cholesterol and of the lipoprotein fractions in the blood may lead to new advances that will decrease the incidence of stroke. The techniques that dissolve fresh clots in the arteries of the heart might be used to dissolve fresh clots that form in arteries to the brain. This vast area is understudied.

Some forms of Alzheimer's disease may have a familial or genetic factor that predisposes a person to the disease. Genetic investigations and genetic engineering may give us important clues that will allow us to detect those individuals who are predisposed. Studies may also point, as they have in some other genetic diseases, to metabolic errors in the brain that are preventable or at least treatable. Regrettably, not enough research is being done in this field.

When injury or disease strikes the brain, large concentrations of naturally occurring chemicals, such as glutamate and dopamine, may be released by cells. The brain is sensitive to these neurotransmitters so that under normal conditions the concentration is held to strict limits with little or no variation. When those limits are exceeded, nerve cell membranes may be impaired. The concentration of calcium ions may be changed and nerve cell death follows. It is possible, although not yet proved, that the reduction of excess glutamate in these instances will prevent the nerve cells from dying. Thus, when a brain injury or a stroke occurs, the introduction of a chemical that inhibits the glutamate might preserve the integrity of the brain cell until adequate circulation can be reestablished. We should be doing more to investigate those possibilities.

The loss of brain cells, especially neurons, from whatever cause, is irreversible because nerve cells do not regenerate. But experiments in rats and mice have shown that a section of brain, such as the temporal lobe on one side, can be removed and replaced with temporal lobe tissue from a mouse or rat embryo.

The first experimenters who performed this technique were curious to find out if they could produce a chemical environment around the embryonic nerve cell transplant that would allow it to survive. To their amazement, they found that the tissue not only survived but reconstituted a bridge to the amputated stump of the adult temporal lobe. Furthermore, the embryonic hippocampal cells in the graft re-formed the very precise and complicated geometric pattern that is present in the adult temporal lobe. Recently, there has even been some indication that the transplanted tissue is reintegrated into the adult nervous system, that is, that the wiring is partially hooked up again so that the tissue becomes functional.

This all sounds very encouraging and it is. Similar fetal brain cell transplants have been performed in the basal ganglia, the pituitary, and the bottom of the brain (hypothalamus) leading to the pituitary. Attempts have been made to reintegrate tissue into the amputated spinal cord. There have been surgical attempts to use these techniques in humans, especially in Parkinson patients. In fact, experiments have already been done in Scandinavia, Mexico City, and Denver. However, there is a long way to go before this procedure can be successfully applied to restock with fetal cells a human brain that has lost tissue from disease or injury.

First, complicated immunological problems exist about putting even fetal brain cells into the amputated, diseased, or injured stump of adult human brain tissue. Second is the problem of adequate blood circulation for the regenerating fetal nerve cells. And enormous biochemical and biophysical problems arise about creating the proper environment for reintegrating the growing fetal nerve cell tissue into the adult brain. Then there is the potential problem of neoplasia (development of tumors) in fetal nerve cell transplants. Many of these cells are so primitive that instead of developing into adult brain cells or brain tissue they may take an alternative biological path and become brain tumors, some of which may be malignant.

Although there are clues to indicate how such transplants might be accomplished, there remains a substantial gap in our knowledge, and it may take many years to solve the problems posed by this technique.

While science forges ahead in the direction of transplants, we must not overlook the overwhelming social and ethical problems involved with these procedures, some of which were discussed in a 1983 national conference that Dr. Tom Sabin and I sponsored. The conference hosted many notable speakers, including a professor of philosophy, Robert Neville; an attorney specializing in medical affairs, William Carnahan; and a conservative Catholic priest, Rev. Paul Murphy, all of whom discussed the moral and ethical concerns of transplant procedures. One issue raised was where the fetal nerve cells are going to come from for human transplants. It has been possible to use cross-species nerve cell transplants in other animals (fetal nerve cells from mouse embryos have been used successfully to reconstitute neural tissue in the adult rat), but it is a much bigger step to suggest that we can use fetal nerve cell transplants from chimpanzees that will not be immunologically rejected by the adult human brain.

Father Murphy accepted the basic premise of the procedure so long as fetal nerve cell material was not gathered in what he considered an unethical fashion. He felt that fetal nerve cells from spontaneous human abortions, so-called miscarriages, would be acceptable from a moral and ethical point of view. However, spontaneous abortions don't occur often enough to supply the amount of brain cell tissue that would be necessary to accommodate future demand. In this country alone probably two and a half million people with Alzheimer's disease are losing brain cells at an inappropriate rate. Furthermore, the products of spontaneous abortions may have damaged brain cells that are inadequate for transplantation.

From basic nutritional research to the moral, ethical, and biological dilemmas posed by fetal nerve cell transplants, we are at an important stage in our understanding of the brain. Our choices of what to investigate will not be easy. Will we spend the millions of dollars needed to develop effective techniques for brain cell transplants, a procedure that theoretically has the potential to make paraplegics walk and Parkinson patients function normally? Or will we spend our resources on ways to improve the future quality of life for children by targeting those projects that hold the most promise for curing genetic diseases? Or can we afford to do both? The future prospect of a major breakthrough in brain research appears bright, but we have far to go, and many crucial decisions will have to be made along the way.

YOUR FUTURE BEGINS TODAY

Whenever a young child comes into my office with a massive head injury because a parent failed to buckle her safely into a car seat, or when I treat a thirty- or forty-year-old alcohol and drug abuser with progressive brain disease, or when I find another nursing home resident who wasted years of his life because someone overmedicated him, I see clearly that the ability for many of us to keep our brain power up is well within our grasp.

The secrets to maintaining and preserving brain power will not be found in high-tech miracle operations or machines. Vast numbers of us can be helped right now by doing relatively simple things: avoiding brain poisons, taking sensible precautions to avoid brain injury, eating properly to avoid strokes and heart disease, which can cause brain dysfunction, and following a regimen of good physical and mental exercises to keep fit and agile.

Medicine has come far in the last few decades in the treatment of disease, but the greatest progress in improving the quality of life is in the area of preventive medicine. Looking back decades from now, medical historians will probably say that our time was remarkable for being the first time in history when large numbers of people discovered the benefits of regular exercise and good nutrition. Improved technology certainly gives us hope that many of the diseases to which we now succumb, like cancer, can eventually be cured. But we also know already that certain cancers (lung cancer, for example) are easily avoidable through simple preventive measures (not smoking).

The most difficult cases I have are not medically oriented but rather deal with problems of attitude. It's the fifty-year-old factory worker who smokes two packs of cigarettes a day, eats high-fat foods, and takes large doses of antihypertensive medications until one day he has a stroke who puts up the most resistance to a change in habits. "Why can't you doctors do something to cure my headaches and vertigo?" he'll say. "Why can't you just prescribe something to make my blackouts go away?" I tell him that he can change his attitude, change his habits, and improve his life and longevity by doing a few simple things. "No," he'll tell me, "I tried that once and it didn't work."

Therein lies the problem: How do you convince someone that mental and physical fitness is a process that continues through a lifetime? "It's too late for me to do those things, Doctor." How do you tell someone that he can make things better by starting in a small way today and continuing every day thereafter?

President Kennedy liked to tell a story about a man who lived on a large estate. One day the man went out to talk to his gardener about planting a rare flowering Japanese tree. He said to the gardener, "When you have a chance, I'd like you to plant it over there, by the ledge, where everyone will be able to see it." The gardener protested. "Don't you know, sir," he said, "that that tree won't bloom for a hundred years?" "In that case," said the man, "plant it today."

The advice I give all who come to me for help is most useful, I tell them, if they start today. The exercises, diets, and other strategies for keeping your brain power at an optimal level work better the longer they're used.

Maybe you're getting older and you say, "Why should I bother? What do I have to gain?" I reply, "Which of us would not be better off with a brain that worked even a little more efficiently?"

Who can refrain from cheering when a cerebral palsy victim is able to make a little paper mobile to hang in her room? Who can be so callous as not to be moved when a man who suffered a stroke is able to communicate again by writing with his left hand? Would you not want to hug someone when he or she begins to speak coherently again after being taken off toxic drugs?

Are these small things? No, not really. In each case the person gained greater control over his or her environment.

The healthier a person's brain, the greater his or her control will be, and the greater the chances will be for a satisfying and meaningful life. Don't wait until tomorrow. Your future begins today.

Appendixes

Bibliography
Index

Mental Status Exams

CHECKING SOMEONE ELSE'S MENTAL STATUS

Part I: General Appearance

1. Does your subject take good care of himself/herself?
   a) No, physical appearance and personal hygiene are very poor.
   b) Yes, general appearance is good, but there are a few problem areas.
   c) Yes, appearance and hygiene are excellent.

2. Does your subject have any obvious nervous problems?
   a) Yes, he/she has an uncontrollable movement disorder or a nervous tic.
   b) Yes, he/she can't seem to sit still.
   c) No, no noticeable problem.

Part II: Mental Inventory

3. Describe your subject's general state of alertness.
   a) He/she seems confused, dazed, or bewildered.
   b) He/she seems listless or dull but basically alert.
   c) He/she seems alert and attentive.

4. Ask your subject where he/she is, what year it is, and what his/her name is.
   a) He/she can't answer any of the questions clearly or correctly.
   b) He/she answers correctly most of the time but makes a few errors.
   c) All correct answers to the questions.

5. Ask your subject where he/she was during the last twenty-four hours and what he/she did.
   a) He/she can't remember any details.
   b) He/she remembers most things but is vague on exact details.
   c) Perfect recall.

Part III: Speech and Language

6. Say the phrase "No ifs, ands, or buts" and ask your subject to repeat it exactly as you said it.
   a) He/she cannot repeat it without making an error.
   b) He/she made a mistake the first time but repeated it correctly the second time.
   c) Perfect recall and pronunciation.

7. Take out a newspaper, magazine, or book and choose a short sentence at random. Read the sentence aloud and ask your subject to write it from memory after he/she hears it once. When he/she is done, compare the original sentence with his/her written version.
   a) There are several mistakes, or the two versions aren't even close.
   b) There are a couple of minor mistakes, but it is basically correct.
   c) Everything is transcribed correctly.

8. Using any five or six objects you have at hand, such as a pen, ring, bracelet, watch, shoe, or metal clasp of a watchband, point to each object in succession and ask your subject to name each one correctly.
   a) He/she is unable to name more than two correctly.
   b) He/she made one or two errors, such as mispronouncing "clasp" as "claps."
   c) Everything was named correctly.

9. Ask your subject to name, from memory, as many animals as he/she can in one minute.
   a) He/she named fewer than 10.
   b) He/she named between 11 and 15 correctly but also made some mistakes in pronunciation or identification.
   c) He/she named more than 16 animals correctly and made no errors.

10. Say the word *world* aloud and ask your subject to spell it backward.
    a) He/she can't spell it correctly at all.
    b) He/she got it right, but only after a second or third try.
    c) He/she spelled it correctly the first time.

Part IV: Motor Functions

11. Ask your subject to put his/her right hand on his/her left ear and then put his/her left hand on his/her right ear.
    a) He/she is unable to carry out the command.
    b) He/she got a little confused but completed the command on the second attempt.
    c) No mistakes.

12. Ask your subject first to use his/her hands to show how he/she would comb his/her hair and then to use his/her hands to show how he/she would tie the laces on his/her shoes.
    a) He/she made several attempts but produced nothing but random or uncoordinated motions.
    b) He/she had trouble with the exercises but was able to complete them.
    c) He/she followed all the commands with ease.

13. Instruct your subject to make a fist with one hand and to use the fist to strike a desk or chair arm. Then instruct him/her to open the fist of the other hand and use the palm to strike a desk or arm chair. Then ask him/her to alternate hands, ten times in rapid succession, between striking with a fist and striking with the palm. Then have him/her reverse hands.
    a) He/she is not able to do the exercise in any sort of coordinated fashion.

b) He/she had some difficulty in doing the exercise but finally did it ten times in good form.

c) He/she had no difficulty with the exercise.

Part V: Higher Intellectual Abilities

14. Without giving your subject any pencil or paper, ask him/her to subtract 16 from 100.
    a) He/she gave a completely wrong answer.
    b) He/she first answered with something like 86, but then realized his/her mistake.
    c) He/she answered correctly.

15. Again without any paper or pencil, ask your subject to add 27 and 14.
    a) He/she was way off.
    b) He/she was wrong but close.
    c) He/she was correct.

16. After a few simple multiplication questions, such as 2×3 and 10×5, start with 12×7 and move gradually up to 12×13.
    a) He/she had trouble with even the simple questions and got none of the twelves correct.
    b) He/she got all the simple questions but had a little difficulty with 12×13.
    c) He/she got everything right.

17. Ask your subject to interpret the following proverbs.
    1) A rolling stone gathers no moss.
    2) A stitch in time saves nine.
    3) A person who lives in a glass house shouldn't throw stones.

    a) He/she interpreted all of them literally and didn't know what they meant.
    b) He/she got one of them wrong.
    c) He/she interpreted all of them correctly.

18. With a paper and pencil, ask your subject to draw a circle to represent the face of a clock and then to write in the numbers around the face, just as they would appear on a clock.
    a) The numbers are all on one side of the clock.

   b) The numbers are in approximately the right places, but there
   are a couple of errors in placement.

   c) The clock face is perfect.

19. Briefly show your subject the following diagram of a house and
ask him/her to draw it without looking at it a second time.

   a) The house is out of proportion, with no depth.

   b) The house is more or less correct, but the details are missing.

   c) The house is in good proportion and all the details are there.

Part VI: Long-Term Memory

20. Ask your subject to name the current president of the United
States and the preceding four in reverse order.

   a) He/she can't recall either the current one or any of the previous four.

   b) He/she made one mistake or did not get the correct order of
the previous four.

   c) He/she made no mistakes.

21. Give your subject one of the following sets of words and tell
him/her to memorize the words. Then go back to question 13
and ask a few more addition, subtraction, and multiplication
questions like those in questions 14–16. Finally, ask your subject
to repeat the set of words, in order.

door, window, and mirror

horse, banana, and Chevrolet

a) He/she cannot recall any of the words or can recall only one word.

b) He/she got two words right but in the wrong order.

c) He/she got all three correct and in the right order.

SCORING

Score 1 point for each (a) response, 2 points for each (b) response, and 3 points for each (c) response. Then add up the totals for the entire test. Use the following simple guide to analyze your subject's score.

58–63: The subject is very likely mentally intact. Where there were errors, they were probably due to a lack of concentration rather than a real deficit.

43–57: The subject appears weak in a few areas. There is definite cause for concern, and a more detailed examination should be done.

Below 43: The subject has obvious mental deficits and needs immediate evaluation by a trained professional.

For this test and the mental status self-exam that follows, it is important to keep track of which questions were answered incorrectly. For example, it's possible that someone could do well on the memory and language parts of the exam, which would indicate that the dominant or left hemisphere is probably adequate, while at the same time scoring below normal in drawing ability and the ability to place numbers correctly on a clock face. The overall score may indicate no cause for concern, but the subject could still have a serious problem in a particular area.

When I score mental status exams, I evaluate them in two ways. First, I see if the overall score is in an acceptable region. Second, I examine whether any specific wrong answers may indicate something out of the ordinary.

CHECKING YOUR OWN MENTAL STATUS

Part I: General Appearance

1. Do you notice that it's more difficult for you to take care of your personal grooming needs than it used to be?

a) Yes, I can't seem to keep myself together anymore.

b) It's a struggle, but I always take care of myself.

c) No, it's no problem.

2. Have you noticed any uncontrollable nervous problems, like a nervous tic or an inability to sit still for more than a minute?

a) Yes, I catch myself making movements I hadn't intended.

b) I don't think I have a problem, but some people say I do.

c) No, there's no problem.

Part II: Mental Inventory

3. Describe your general state of alertness.

a) I have trouble staying alert much of the time.

b) I sometimes feel a little listless or dull.

c) I've never noticed any problem with alertness.

4. Can you recall what you had to eat yesterday?

a) I can't remember anything I had to eat.

b) I can recall a couple of meals, but not all.

c) I remember exactly what I ate.

Part III: Speech and Language

5. Say the following phrase out loud: "No ifs, ands, or buts." Did you have any trouble saying it?

a) I had a lot of problems saying the words.

b) I had a little trouble, but I did say it.

c) I had no trouble.

6. Name as many animals as you can in one minute. Time yourself on a clock with a second hand.

a) I named 5 to 10 animals.

b) I named 11 to 15 animals.

c) I named more than 16 animals.

Part IV: Motor Functions

7. When you got up this morning, did you comb your hair, tie your shoes, and button your shirt by yourself with no assistance?

a) No, I needed help.
b) Yes, but I had some trouble.
c) Yes, I had no trouble.

Part V: Higher Intellectual Abilities

8. Without using a pencil to calculate, write down the answers to
   the following math questions:
   1) 90 minus 16
   2) 37 plus 14
   3) 12 times 7
   4) 12 times 11
   5) 12 times 13

   a) I got three or more wrong answers.
   b) I got one or two wrong answers, but only in the multiplication
      problems.
   c) I got all the answers correct.

Part VI: Long-Term Memory

9. Without looking in a reference book, write down the names of
   the last five presidents of the United States, in reverse order,
   starting with the current president.
   a) I could only remember one or two correctly.
   b) I remembered all the presidents, but I had the wrong order.
   c) I had them all right and in the right order.

Answers to Selected Questions
8. 1) 74   2) 51   3) 84   4) 132   5) 156
9. George Bush, Ronald Reagan, Jimmy Carter, Gerald Ford, Richard
   Nixon

SCORING

Score 1 point for each (a) response, 2 points for each (b) response, and
3 points for each (c) response. Add up all the points and check your
score against the following ranges.

25–27: You probably don't notice any problems in your own mental function. This does not necessarily mean that there aren't any problems, but since you're not aware of any you should feel fairly positive about your functioning.

20–25: You seem to have a weak area or two, which may indicate a problem. I suggest you ask someone to administer the longer mental status exam to you and score your results.

Below 20: You definitely have a problem that you should look into. I urge you to have a complete mental status exam, conducted by someone else. If the results are in the lowest range on that exam, you should see a neurologist.

The Brain Power
Exercise Program

The following sets of brain exercises can be used as a supplement to the brain exercises presented in Chapter 12.

PART I: ATTENTION

This set of exercises requires two people, the subject and the examiner. The subject should have a stopwatch and be seated at a table facing the examiner. The examiner should have a pencil and a piece of paper.

Exercise 1

The examiner should pick an increment of time at random, such as 19 seconds, say it out loud, write it down, and then ask the subject to start and then stop the watch at precisely 19 seconds. This same exercise should be repeated three or four times, using different intervals such as 45 seconds, 90 seconds, 29 seconds.

Exercise 2

The examiner should take a piece of paper and tear it up into as many as ten small pieces. On each piece he or she should write a letter of the alphabet and then mentally assign each letter a time value under 60 seconds. For example, *A* may be equal to 25 seconds, *B* 10 seconds, and so on. The examiner should record the letters and values on a separate piece of paper out of sight of the subject.

Once the information is written down, the examiner should show the letters to the subject one at a time and tell him or her the value of each letter. The subject can take as long as a few minutes to memorize the letters and values. When the subject has finished memorizing, the examiner should hold up a letter at random and then ask the subject to start the watch and then stop it at the time equal to the value of the letter.

The examiner might start by giving the subject just four or five letters and times to memorize and then gradually adding more times as the subject gets better at the exercise. The goal is to do a set of six perfectly and then extend that to twelve and finally eighteen.

A variation of this exercise is to use symbols, such as a square, a cube, a triangle, and so on, instead of letters. A triangle might represent 20 seconds, a square 35 seconds, and so forth. It is also possible to use both letters and symbols and to alternate showing them to the subject.

Exercise 3

This exercise improves time estimation skills. The examiner should pick a number between 1 and 60 and ask the subject to start the watch and then, without looking, to stop it at the time he or she thinks corresponds to the time the examiner gave. If the examiner calls out the number 24, the subject would start the watch, wait for what he or she feels is 24 seconds, and then stop the watch.

The examiner should keep track of the number called out and the actual value picked by the subject so that the subject can see progress in estimating time. This exercise should be practiced until the subject can accurately stop the watch at intervals up to one minute without looking.

Exercise 4

The examiner should either put a copy of this book in front of the subject or should reproduce a block of random letters and numbers such as the following. The examiner should ask the subject to circle in pencil every 4 and every *g* in the block in no more than 15 seconds.

a 7 3 d g t p 9 6 2 x d e o e w q d c 5 6 0 1

d g v c d w 3 6 7 9 w d z x j g e 2 3 7 b f d

x c k l p o u t e e 4 c v b n m s w e r u i o

p h 4 f d s a q w 6 r t y u i 7 o e r t y u i

4 d e r g f r t y u i c s w r d w 2 5 3 4 4 d

3 s w e d 3 5 h t c e 3 c d f g h y w s q x d

In this block there are five 4's and five *g*'s. If the subject is not able to find them in 15 seconds, the examiner should erase the marks already made and ask the subject to look for *c*'s and 5's in 15 seconds. There are seven *c*'s and three 5's. If the subject is not able to do this, the examiner should choose another letter and number combination and repeat the exercise three or four more times.

PART II: MEMORY

You can improve recall in a number of ways, most of which involve using strong images to keep track of objects. I present two methods here, the peg system and acronym building.

Peg System

The peg system creates a set of memory aids out of familiar objects. Choose any ten objects that have strong visual associations for you. You might choose a Garfield doll, a sports car, a baseball bat, and so on. Once you have your list, memorize the ten items, associating with each item a number from 1 to 10, in order. Suppose that number 1 is Garfield, number 2 a sports car, and number 3 a baseball bat. Those ten objects are called pegs. Anytime you need to remember anything in a list — a grocery list, names at a meeting — you can use the pegs to help your memory.

Suppose you need ten items at the grocery store, including cereal, soap powder, and skim milk. To remember your list you can associate each grocery item with one of the already-memorized pegs. Using our example, you would associate Garfield with a box of cereal (perhaps by visualizing Garfield eating a bowl of cereal), a sports car with soap powder (maybe by imagining a sports car in a giant tub filled with soap powder), and a baseball bat with skim milk (perhaps by imagining that the bat is a straw in a glass of the milk).

The object is to think of an unusual image that will link the object you need to remember with one of your pegs. The more ridiculous or emotionally charged the images are, the easier they will be to picture and remember.

Acronym Building

Another way to remember lists of objects is to use acronyms, which are new words formed from the initial letters of a series of words. For example, WAC is the acronym for Women's Army Corps.

To help you remember a list, you can create any new word that has some meaning to you and that contains the first letters of the names of objects on your list. If you need to remember to buy tomatoes, cauliflower, and lettuce, you might come up with the acronym TLC, for "tender loving care" and "tomatoes, lettuce, and cauliflower."

Sometimes the list of words you need to remember does not form any easily identifiable acronym. In such cases you can create a nonsense sentence, known as an acrostic, in which the first letter of each word stands for one of the words in your list. It helps if the sentence contains a strong image. If your list of words is fireplace, radio, alarm, patron, and desk, you can make up a sentence like "*First Place Receives A Dime.*"

In medical school, my classmates and I learned the cranial nerves in the following way. The nerves are olfactory, optic, oculomotor, trochlear, trigeminal, abducens, facial, acoustic, glossopharyngeal, vagus, spinal accessory, and hypoglossal. We used the acrostic "On Old Olympus *Towering Top A Finn And German Vend Some Hops.*"

Certain words and phrases sometimes remind us of song melodies, and it's possible to systematically make this association work for us in remembering things. If you need to have your car repaired, for example, you could use the familiar line "Row, row, row your boat gently down the stream" and singing or humming "Fix, fix, fix the car just as soon as possible."

To make use of this process, choose a familiar song that you easily remember. You could select the national anthem, for example, or perhaps a favorite hymn or popular song. Whatever it is, it should be one you have fixed in your mind.

PART III: REMEMBERING NUMBERS

Many numbers, such as telephone numbers, occur randomly and it's not easy to keep them straight. Generally, the bigger or longer the number, the more difficult it is to remember. There are a couple of ways to get around this problem.

First, you can try converting a long number like 1529 into dollars and cents: $15.29. A number like 35,072 would become $350.72.

What if you are presented with a telephone number such as 862-3481? You can split the phone number into two parts, 862 and 3481, and convert those parts to dollars and cents: $8.62 and $34.81.

PART IV: MATHEMATICAL ABILITIES

We've all become so used to calculators and computers by now that many of us have forgotten how to do even simple arithmetic. From our brain's point of view, that is unfortunate because using mathematics can help us keep our agility at a high level.

There is no way to improve mathematical ability without actually doing math. The easiest and most painless way to keep in practice is to balance your checkbook without the aid of a calculator. You can always check your math afterward, but actually doing all the addition and subtraction will be beneficial.

You should also practice doing some relatively simple addition, subtraction, multiplication, and division exercises with a stopwatch. You might try this simple test in 30 seconds:

$$123 + 248 =$$
$$293 - 215 =$$
$$24 \times 345 =$$
$$48 \div 6 =$$
$$386 + 294 =$$

If those are too easy for you, you can make up some sets of your own and check your answers with a calculator. It is important that the problems be done in a specified time limit and that they be done accurately. After doing these kinds of problems for a couple of minutes each day, you should begin to see some improvement in your skill level after about two weeks.

PART V: COMPLEX VISUAL PROCESSING

One of the first things children learn to do in kindergarten and nursery school is to copy drawings and color them in. As it happens, copying drawings is an excellent way to exercise the nondominant hemisphere, and it can be used as an aid to developing ambidexterity.

The drawings you should practice copying (see pages 222–226) are not pictures; they don't represent anything specifically. They are mainly straight lines that intersect at different angles.

Keep in mind that no one can draw a perfectly straight line without the use of a ruler. What you are trying to achieve with these drawings is a better spatial-visual sense. You should notice where the lines intersect one another and how long the lines are in relation to other lines.

Use your right hand (whether you are left- or right-handed) to do the copying. Using a stopwatch, give yourself 90 seeconds to do all five on a separate piece of paper.

After that, try using your left hand to do the same drawings. Again allot 90 seconds to do all of them.

If you're really energetic, you can try doing all the drawings from memory and then compare them to the originals. Doing this exercise is useful not only for spatial-visual acuity but also for memory and attention.

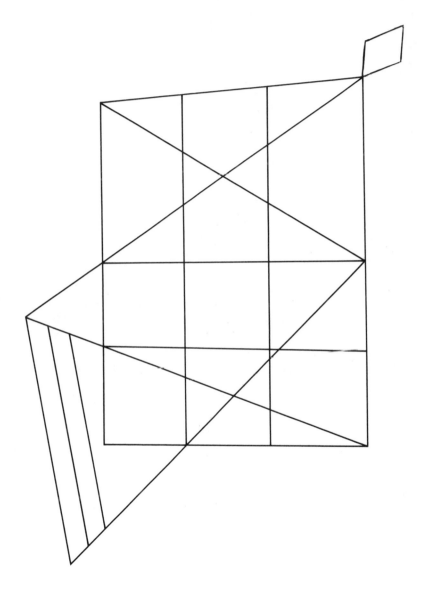

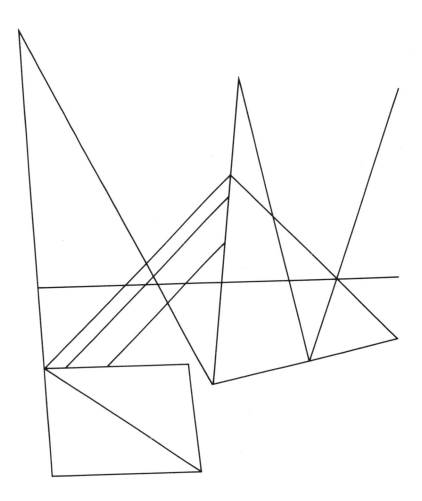

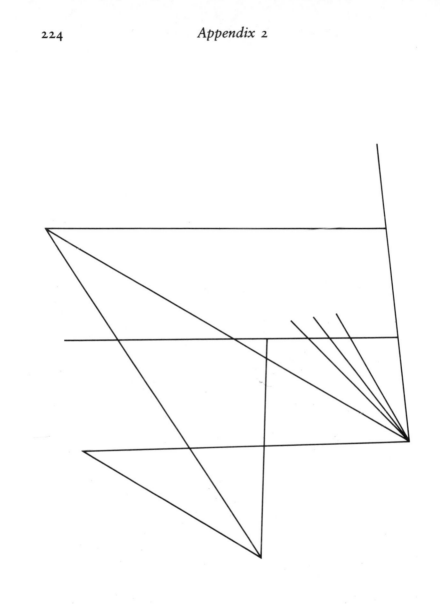

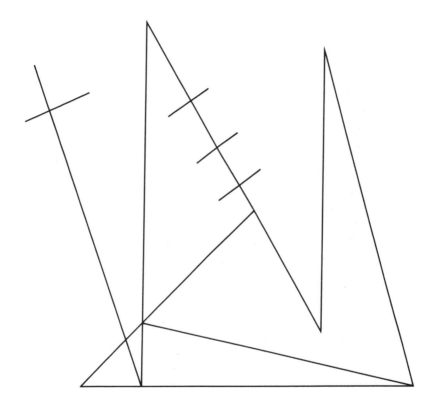

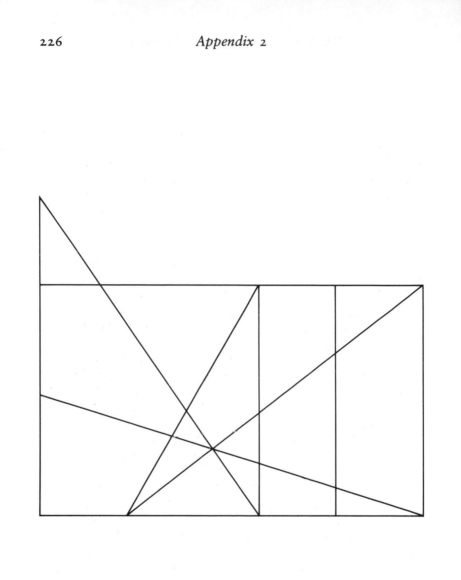

PART VI: HANDEDNESS EXERCISES

In addition to drawing figures with your left hand if you're right-handed (or with your right hand if you are a dominant left-hander), you should also try writing letters and words with your left hand (with your right hand if you are left-handed). A blackboard is the best writing surface for these exercises because you can write with large letters. However, it's quite possible to practice handedness exercises with a paper and pencil.

Try not to put too much pressure on the chalk or pen or pencil. At first, you'll probably have some difficulty forming recognizable letters, and your difficulty may cause you to tense up and try harder. Don't do that. You will quickly get frustrated and lose interest.

Start slowly, spending about three to five minutes a day writing the alphabet from *A* to *Z*. After you can do that well, use a stopwatch and try doing it again in less than 15 seconds. If you can do that ten times, then call it quits for the day and try again tomorrow.

After you master the alphabet, try copying the following phrases:

The spry old man ran down the side of the road.
The gray dog chased the small red fox across the green field.
The large policeman with a black mustache handcuffed the frightened criminal.
The dappled chestnut mare easily jumped the stone wall.
The Royal Irish constabulary extinguished the conflagration.

With practice, you should be able to copy each sentence in less than 10 seconds.

The object of these lessons is to increase your familiarity and comfort in writing with your left hand. To become truly ambidextrous you will have to write left-handed during your regular workday, getting to the point where it feels comfortable to use your left hand to take notes or do paperwork.

To get to this stage, however, may take many months of practice, but if you are conscientious and do some exercises for a few minutes each day, before you know it you'll be well on your way.

Appendix 3

Commonly Asked Questions About Brain Power

FOODS AND DIETS

QUESTION: You imply that a high-protein diet, which contains essential amino acids such as tyrosine, will improve my ability to concentrate and be alert in business situations that are challenging and require maximum efficiency on my part. Yet I've noticed in the past that when I eat steak, which certainly contains a lot of protein, I have not felt alert. Can you explain this?

ANSWER: The better cuts of steak contain not only a lot of protein but also substantial amounts of hard fat. This fat has two detrimental properties. First, it tends to promote atherosclerosis. Second, it delays the stomach's emptying time, increases the period of digestion and subsequently absorption, and is associated with lassitude and mental dullness.

You do not want to feel dull if you are confronting a challenging situation that requires utmost mental agility. What you need are the kinds of meals described in Chapter 11. They concentrate on chicken and turkey, which don't contain much fat.

QUESTION: My daughter and her husband are strict vegetarians. They both seem to me to be listless and lacking in energy all the time. Is there anything in their diet that could account for this?

ANSWER: Yes, vegetarians can be vulnerable to deficiencies. In particular, one essential B vitamin that is lacking in all vegetarian diets is vitamin B_{12}, essential ingredient in the myelination process in the brain. It is also easy for vegetarians to take in too little folate, and this deficiency can result in pernicious anemia and spinal cord diseases.

There is nothing wrong with being a strict vegetarian so long as the essential vitamins, minerals, and amino acids are ingested through daily supplements.

QUESTION: My fifty-six-year-old father had a heart attack. The doctor told him that his blood pressure is somewhat elevated, and I'm worried that he might have a stroke. Is there anything that we can do to prevent this?

ANSWER: There is an increased chance that your father is susceptible to stroke, and you can do a few things to prevent this. First, his blood pressure must be brought down to the normal range. If it's only slightly elevated, bringing it down may be accomplished by restricting salt in his diet. If it's substantially elevated, he may require antihypertensive medication.

Your father should also be on a low-fat diet, not one that merely reduces his cholesterol but one that increases the high-density lipoproteins (HDLs) that circulate in his bloodstream.

There is some indication that changing his diet and reducing both the cholesterol and the low-density lipoproteins will actually cause an improvement in his arterial disease that caused his heart attack and that might contribute to a stroke.

Finally, it's important for your doctor to determine if there are any sources of little clots that could break off and float into your father's brain circulation. Clots that are especially apt to do this originate from diseased tissue in the lining of the great blood vessels (carotid arteries) in the neck that go to the brain. He might be a candidate to have medication that will reduce the chance of this happening.

If the risk is only slight, a drug like aspirin might be effective in preventing clots associated with the clumping of blood platelets. Or he may need more effective anticlotting medication. Since these medications also increase the chance of bleeding, he must use them efficiently and only under medical supervision.

BRAIN POWER EXERCISES

QUESTION: In your brain power exercise program you emphasize training the nondominant hand in skilled behavior, for example, trying to write with your left hand if you're predominantly right-handed. Is there any way of training the nondominant hemisphere to receive verbal or written messages, and can a method for this kind of language training be incorporated into the brain power exercise program?

ANSWER: Yes, there are methods of subjecting the nondominant hemisphere to both verbal and written language. One method is called dichotic listening. The subject has earphones placed into each ear like those worn by a stenographer or like the earpieces of a doctor's stethoscope. The sound transmission into one ear can be cut off so that the verbal messages go into only one ear.

There are also different kinds of apparatus that shut out the images to one visual field so that written images can be seen in only one visual field and go to only one hemisphere.

Unfortunately, at this point the apparatus used for both these techniques is beyond the scope of this book. They certainly are powerful learning tools for both language and other kinds of messages such as those contained in music or pictures.

QUESTION: I'm a schoolteacher and I am using various intellectual faculties continuously to teach my students. Why do I need to do mental agility exercises?

ANSWER: As a teacher, you may be concentrating on one set of subjects, like mathematics or literature, while neglecting others. That is why the mental agility program includes a wider range of activities than you would ordinarily use in your job.

ALZHEIMER'S DISEASE AND DEPRESSION

QUESTION: My father, age sixty-one, retired a few months ago after being on the job for forty-two years. Since that time he's been staying at home almost all the time, and for days on end he won't get out of bed.

When I ask him what's wrong he says, "Nothing." He doesn't seem depressed to me, but I'm afraid there is some problem. What should I do? ANSWER: Relatives of someone who has worked for forty-two years and then retires are often tempted to say, "Well, let him be. He's worked long enough, let him do what he wants to do." For many people, the necessity and discipline of work are the central theme around which their life revolves. Take it away and it creates a vacuum. Their life ceases to have meaning, and they become clinically depressed.

The body needs to be used. Exercise is necessary or the limbs become stiff, the muscles atrophied, and the bones decalcified. In a similar way, the brain needs to be used. If it lies fallow, its efficiency decreases. My advice is to first get a medical and neurological evaluation for your father: medical, because serious illness may also announce itself for the first time by sudden depression; neurological, because a number of brain problems mimic this clinical syndrome. Psychotherapy or antidepressant drug treatment may be necessary.

However, before starting on the medical route, try to get your father interested and involved in some aspect of his environment. Maybe you could enlist the aid of some of his friends and neighbors. If this fails, seek professional evaluation.

BRAIN POISONS

QUESTION: I am thirty-five and a recovering alcoholic and drug addict. I was an alcohol abuser for twenty years and a drug addict for ten years. Recently I've been diagnosed as having manic-depressive syndrome and have been controlled on antidepressant medication and lithium. Did the alcohol and drugs make me more depressed, or was I born with this disability?
ANSWER: It's impossible to know, without taking a family history, but some patients with manic-depressive illness have a strong familial tendency to develop this disorder. People who are depressed are much more susceptible to taking alcohol or drugs, like cocaine, in a vain effort to treat their depression. Of course, it never works. Cocaine is a very poor drug to take because it produces a depression during withdrawal that is worse than the original depression. Alcohol is also a

brain depressant. The chronic intake of both these brain poisons only makes the depression worse.

It is very important for people with a manic-depressive disorder to be accurately diagnosed so that they can receive effective treatment. They must also understand that brain poisons like alcohol, cocaine, and other drugs are just going to put them in a spiral of increasing depression and brain dysfunction.

QUESTION: My sixty-two-year-old husband has for many years smoked a pack and a half a day. He's a supervisor in a plant, and recently he's been having difficulty doing his job. He says that the paperwork is murder. Could his problems be related to his smoking habit?

ANSWER: Yes, smoking could be related to his problems on the job. Cigarette smoking adversely affects the brain in a number of ways. First, nicotine is a brain stimulant and is quite habit-forming. When people try to stop smoking, they may notice a change in their behavior from withdrawal symptoms.

Second, chronic cigarette smoking tends to be associated with obstructive pulmonary disease, and it tends to make preexisting lung conditions such as asthma worse. If your husband is becoming short of breath or if his lips and fingernails are sometimes blue, his brain may not be getting enough oxygen.

Nicotine also has an adverse affect on the blood vessels and the capillary circulation. It is one of the factors associated with an increased incidence of coronary disease, and I believe that it also has a tendency to diminish blood flow to the brain.

Finally, cigarette smoking is associated with lung cancer, one of the cancers that most frequently spreads to the brain. If your husband has asthmatic attacks and is on a medication like aminophylline, the medicine itself can have an adverse effect on brain function.

BRAIN INJURY AND DISEASE

QUESTION: My two-year-old infant daughter seems to get hit repeatedly on the head. She falls down and hits her head, she strikes her head on the edge of her playpen, she bangs her head on the crib, and so on. Does this mean that she's going to be brain-damaged because of these repeated head injuries? And what can I do about it?

ANSWER: Repeated trivial head injuries are commonplace in two-, three-, and even four-year-old children, and there is no evidence that injuries of the sort you describe have any permanent effect on the brain or brain function.

The reasons for this are several. First, the force and the changes in acceleration are quite small. Second, in normal two-to-four-year-olds, there is little space between the brain and the cranium. The brain is surrounded by a cushion of spinal fluid and it has a cushion of spinal fluid within it. Those cushions are an effective shock-absorbing mechanism that soaks up the energy of trivial head trauma without causing any brain damage.

However, a head injury that causes even a momentary loss of consciousness or a change in behavior afterward would be classified not as trivial but as minor and would require an evaluation of brain function.

If the number of falls and head injuries is excessive, your doctor might ask some questions: Is your child's brain development occurring at a normal rate? Is she unusually clumsy in coordinating movements and in sustaining balance? And, finally, are the head injuries the result of minor lapses in consciousness such as could be caused by minor seizures (petit mal seizures)? The latter can be determined by neurological examination associated with specific tests like brain wave tests.

QUESTION: My fifteen-year-old niece has epileptic seizures that don't seem to be controlled by medicine. She's not doing well in school and her social life is not good. What can she do?

ANSWER: If her epileptic seizures are uncontrolled, they certainly may have hurt her performance in school. Since the seizures may be associated with confusion and loss of memory, new learning may be difficult.

The first thing to do is to get a good diagnosis of where her seizures are coming from. If they are not well controlled, she may be having seizures from her temporal lobe, which may require a different kind of medication than she is now receiving.

Once her seizures are controlled, she may find new confidence for improving her social life.

QUESTION: My mother died of a brain tumor, and I've been having headaches recently, the same kind of headaches that she had when her trouble started. What should I do?

ANSWER: There is no evidence that the great majority of brain tumors are inherited or even familial, although a small minority do tend to run in families. Since you are having symptoms, you should have a neurological examination and other appropriate tests. A CAT scan or magnetic resonance scan should be able to rule out the possibility of a brain tumor and relieve your anxiety on that score.

Sometimes anxiety and the depression it produces can cause a substantial change in one's ability to think and perform. A normal brain scan can be most valuable under these circumstances.

QUESTION: My seventeen-year-old niece has cerebral palsy. She has difficulty forming her words and is severely restricted in her movement. Does this mean that she's mentally retarded, and can this condition be inherited?

ANSWER: No, she is probably not mentally retarded. Cerebral palsy is usually caused by a lack of oxygen to the brain during the time of birth. It is not an inherited condition. Cerebral palsy victims may appear to be demented because they have such difficulty speaking, and of course their ability to move their arms and legs is severely hampered.

I've examined hundreds of people with cerebral palsy and I've been surprised that they have relatively preserved intellectual function. This makes it quite important to persevere with physical, occupational, and speech therapy.

One cerebral palsy patient wrote me quite intelligent letters on a typewriter using the great toe of her right foot to punch the keys. Because her brain function was preserved, she was able to lead a relatively normal life by making adjustments for her disability. I encourage all families of the sufferers of this disorder to get as much help as they can from cerebral palsy organizations.

Bibliography

Adams, R. D., and Victor, M. *Principles of Neurology,* 3rd edition. McGraw-Hill, New York, 1985.

Andreason, N. C. *The Broken Brain.* Harper & Row, New York, 1984.

Barnes, H. N., Aronson, M. D., and Delbanco, T. L., eds. *Alcoholism: A Guide for the Primary Care Physician.* Springer-Verlag, New York, 1987. (See especially Chapter 1, pp. 3–46, and Chapter 4, "The Clinical Pharmacology of Alcohol" by Fox, Guzman, and Friedman.)

Beaton, G. H., and Bengoa, J. M., eds. *Nutrition in Preventive Medicine.* World Health Organization, Geneva, 1976.

Benton, D., and Roberts, G. "Effects of Vitamin and Mineral Supplements on Intelligence of a Sample of School Children." *The Lancet,* Vol. 1, No. 8578, January 23, 1988, pp. 140–143.

Buell, S. V., and Coleman, P. D. "Dendritic Growth in the Aged Human Brain in Senile Dementia." *Science,* Vol. 206, 1979, pp. 854–856.

Davidoff, D. A., Kessler, H. R., Laibstain, D. F., and Mark, V. H. "Neurobehavioral Sequelae of Minor Head Injury: A Consideration of Post-Concussive Syndrome Versus Past Traumatic Stress Disorder." *Cognitive Rehabilitation,* March/April 1988, pp. 8–13.

DeRopp, R. S. *Drugs and the Mind.* Grove Press, New York, 1957.

Driesbach, R. H., and Robertson, W. *Handbook of Poisoning.* Appleton and Lange, Norwalk, 1987.

Edwards, T. "The Right Food Means Brighter Children." BBC broadcast, reprinted in *New Community: Journal of the Commission for Racial Equality,* Vol. 14, No. 1/2, 1987.

Gawin, F. H., and Ellingwood, E. H. "Cocaine and Other Stimulants." *New England Journal of Medicine,* Vol. 318, No. 18, May 5, 1988, pp. 1173–1182.

Gildenberg, P. L., Mark, V. H., and Regelson, W., eds. *Proceedings of the Colloquium on the Use of Embryonic Cell Transplantation for Correction of CNS Disorders.* Chestnut Hill, Mass., June 27–29, 1983. (Sponsored by American Paralysis Association and Sabin & Mark.) *Applied Neurophysiology,* Vol. 47, Nos. 1 and 2, 1984. (The entire volume contains papers presented at this symposium.)

Griffith, H. W. *Complete Guide to Vitamins, Minerals, and Supplements.* Fisher Books, Tucson, 1988.

Harrell, R. F. "Mental Response to Added Thiamine." *J. Nutrition,* Vol. 31, 1946, pp. 283–298.

Hilton, H. *The Executive Memory Guide.* Simon & Schuster, New York, 1986.

Horn, J. L. "Psychometric Studies of Aging and Intelligence." In *Aging: Genesis and Treatment of Psychological Disorders in the Elderly,* edited by Gersons and Rankin, pp. 19–43. Raven Press, New York, 1975.

Katzman, R., and Terry, R. D., eds. *The Neurology of Aging.* F. A. Davis, Philadelphia, 1984.

Lipton, M. A., Mailman, R. B., and Nemeroff, C. B. "Vitamins, Megavitamin Therapy, and the Nervous System." In *Nutrition and the Brain,* edited by Wurtman and Wurtman, p. 183. Raven Press, New York, 1979.

Madrazo, L. V., Torres, C., et al. "Transplantation of Fetal Substantia Nigra and Adrenal Medulla to the Caudate Nucleus in Two Patients with Parkinson's Disease." *New England Journal of Medicine,* Vol. 318, 1988, p. 51.

Mark, V. H. "Sociobiological Theories of Abnormal Aggression." In *Violence: Perspectives on Murder and Aggression,* edited by I. L. Kutash, S. B. Kutash, and L. B. Schlesinger. Jossey-Bass, San Francisco, 1978.

Mark, V. H., and Ervin, F. R. "Relief of Pain by Stereotactic Surgery." In *Pain and the Neurosurgeon: A Forty Year Experience,* edited by White and Sweet, pp. 843–887. C. C. Thomas, Springfield, 1969.

Mark, V. H., and Ervin, F. R. *Violence and the Brain.* Harper & Row, New York, 1970. (See especially "The Either/Or Philosophy," pp. 138–145.)

Mark, V. H., Takada, H., Tsutsumi, H., Takamatsu, E., Toth, E., and Mark, D. B. "Effect of Exogenous Catecholamines in the Amygdala of a 'Rage' Cat." *Applied Neurophysiology,* Vol. 38, 1975, pp. 61–72.

Mark, V. H., and Tsutsumi, H. "The Suppression of Pain by Intrathalamic Lidocaine." In *Advances in Neurology,* Vol. 4, pp. 715–772. Raven Press, New York, 1974.

Meier, M. J., Benton, A., and Diller, L., eds. *Neuropsychological Rehabilitation.* Guilford Press, New York, 1987. (See especially Chapter 5, "Individual Differences in Neuropsychological Recovery" by Meier et al.; Chapter 8, "A Systematic Method for Ameliorating Disorders in Basic Attention" by Benyishay et al.; Chapter 9, "Cognitive Theories of Attention and the Rehabilitation of Attentional Defects" by Posner et al.; Chapter 12, "Rehabilitation of Organic Memory Disorders" by O'Connor et al.; Chapter 13, "Recent Developments in Learning and Memory: Implications for Rehabilitation of the Amnesic Patient" by Salmon et al.; Chapter 14, "Approaches to Neuropsychological Rehabilitation: Language Disorders" by Basso; and Chapter 15, "Neurolinguistic Principles and Aphasia Therapy" by Goodglass.

Mesulam, M.-M., ed. *Principles of Behavioral Neurology.* F. A. Davis, Philadelphia, 1988. (See especially Chapter 2, "Mental State Assessment of Young and Elderly Adults in Behavioral Neurology" by Weintraub and Mesulam; Chapter 3, "Attention, Confusional States, and Neglect" by Mesulam; Chapter 4, "Memory and Amnesias" by Signoret; Chapter 5, "Aphasia and Related Disorders: A Clinical Approach" by Benson and Geschwind.)

Passmore, R., and Eastwood, M. A. *Davidson and Passmore Human Nutrition and Dietetics.* Churchill Livingstone, New York, 1986.

Pearlman, A. L., and Collins, R. C., eds. *Neurological Pathophysiology.* Oxford University Press, New York, 1984.

Pennington, J., and Church, H. *Bowes & Church's Food Values of Portions Commonly Used,* 14th edition. J. B. Lippincott, Philadelphia, 1985.

Robin, H. S., and Michelson, J. B. *Illustrated Handbook of Drug Abuse: Recognition and Diagnosis.* Yearbook Medical Publisher, Chicago, 1988.

Sabin, T. D. "Dementia in the Elderly: Identifying Reversibility." *Hospital Practise,* Nov. 30, 1986.

Sabin, T. D., Vitug, A. J., and Mark, V. H. "Are Nursing Home Diagnoses and Treatment Inadequate?" *J. of the American Medical Association,* Vol. 248, No. 3, July 16, 1982, pp. 321–322.

Salzman, C. *Clinical Geriatric Psychopharmacology.* McGraw-Hill, New York, 1984.

Stevens, J. R., Mark, V. H., Ervin, F., Pacheco, P., and Suematsu, K. "Deep Temporal Stimulation in Man." *Archives of Neurology,* Vol. 21, 1969, pp. 157–169. (Shows the effects of cocaine on deep temporal lobe structures by direct recording.)

Strub, R. L., and Black, F. W. *The Mental Status Examination in Neurology,* 2nd edition. F. A. Davis, Philadelphia, 1987.

Tsutsumi, H., and Mark, V. H. "Experimental Local Thalamic Application of Xylocaine Through Silicone Rubber Chemode." *J. Neurosurgery,* Vol. 38, June 1973, pp. 743–747.

Turney, M. C., Fisher, R. H., Lewis, A. J., Zorzitto, M. G., Snow, W. G., et al. "The NINCPS-ARDRA Work Group Criteria for the Clinical Diagnosis of Probable Alzheimer Disease." *Neurology,* Vol. 38, March 1988, p. 359.

Venna, N., Sabin, T. D., Ordia, J. I., and Mark, V. H. "Treatment of Severe Parkinson's Disease by Intraventricular Injection of Dopamine." *Applied Neurophysiology,* Vol. 47, 1984, pp. 62–64.

Wurtman, J. *Managing Your Mind and Mood Through Food.* Harper & Row, New York, 1986.

Wurtman, R. J., Corkin, S., Frowdon, J. H., and Ritter-Wolker, E., eds. *Alzheimer's Disease.* Proceedings of the Fifth Meeting of the International Study Group on the Pharmacology of Memory Disorders Associated with Aging. Zurich, Switzerland, January 20–22, 1989.

Wurtman, R., and Wurtman, J. eds. *Nutrition and the Brain* (series). Raven Press, New York. Vol. 1: Wurtman and Wurtman, eds. *Determinants of the Availability of Nutrients in the Brain,* 1977. Vol. 5: Barbeau, Growdon, and Wurtman, eds. *Choline and Lecithin in Brain Disorders,* 1979. (Note especially in this volume: Sitaram, N., Weingartner, H., and Gillin, J. C., "Choline Chloride and Acetylcholine: Effects on Memory and Sleep in Man," pp. 367ff.) Vol. 6: Wurtman and Wurtman, eds. *Physiological and Behavior Effects of Food Constituents,* 1987. Vol. 7: Wurtman and Wurtman, eds. *Food Constituents Affecting Normal and Abnormal Behavior,* 1986.

Yakovlev, P. I. "Morphological Criteria of Growth and Maturation of the Nervous System in Man." In *Mental Retardation,* edited by L. G. Kolb, R. I. Maseland, and R. E. Cooke, Vol. 39, pp. 3–46 (research publication of the Association for Research in Nervous and Mental Disease). Williams and Williams, Baltimore, 1962.

Zager, E. L., and Black, P. M. "Neural Transplantation." *Surgical Neurology,* Vol. 29, 1988, pp. 350–366.

NOTE ON VITAMIN AND MINERAL SUPPLEMENTS

Vitamin and mineral supplements can be obtained at your pharmacy. The Schiff Company (121 Moonachie Avenue, Moonachie, N.J. 07074) has put the vitamins and minerals recommended in this book as optimal in one package. The formula can be purchased at most health food stores. The choline can be bought separately at small cost, but I recommend buying the slightly more expensive phosphatidyl choline because it does not give you a "fishy" odor, as choline docs. This can be purchased at most health food stores or directly from Pharmacaps, Inc., 1111 Jefferson Avenue, Elizabeth, N.J. 07201. The brand name is PhosChol®.

Index